LITERACY AND SOCIAL INCLUSION:
CLOSING THE GAP

LITERACY AND SOCIAL INCLUSION:
CLOSING THE GAP

Edited by Eve Bearne
and Jackie Marsh

Trentham Books
Stoke on Trent, UK and Sterling USA

Trentham Books Limited
Westview House   22883 Quicksilver Drive
734 London Road   Sterling
Oakhill   VA 20166-2012
Stoke on Trent   USA
Staffordshire
England ST4 5NP

First published 2007

British Library Cataloguing-in-Publication Data
A catalogue record for this book is available from the
British Library

ISBN-13: 978 1 85856 389 3

Cover: Photograph of Street art in Granada, Spain
by Jackie Marsh

Designed and typeset by Trentham Print Design Ltd,
Chester and printed in Great Britain by Hobbs the
Printers Ltd, Hampshire

Contents

About the Contributors

Eve Bearne divides her time at the University of Cambridge Faculty of Education, UK, between research and teaching. Her current research interests are children's production of multimodal texts and gender, language and literacy. Most recently she was a member of the research team for the Department for Education and Skills project *Raising Boys' Achievement* and with Teresa Grainger co-directed the United Kingdom Literacy Association/Primary National Strategy research and intervention project *Raising Boys' Achievement in Writing*. She has edited several books about diversity, literacy and about children's literature, including *Where Texts and Children Meet: Literature Past, Present and Future* (1999, co-edited with Watson) and *Art, Narrative and Childhood* (2003, co-edited with Styles). She is immediate Past President of the United Kingdom Literacy Association and a Fellow of the English Association.

Viv Bird is an experienced adult and family literacy practitioner and former editor of *Literacy Today* magazine. Viv is also the author of several literacy guides and many articles. In 2002, she became director of the Literacy and Social Inclusion Project, a three-year Basic Skills Agency national support project delivered by the National Literacy Trust, UK. She was responsible for setting up a website (www. literacytrust.org.uk/socialinclusion). With Rodie Akerman, she wrote a position paper 'Every which way we can' launched at the Institute of Education in London in February 2005. A practical handbook, published in November 2005, describes how, working in partnership, policymakers can develop a community literacy strategy with positive outcomes for individuals, families and communities. Viv has recently been appointed as director of Reading Is Fundamental, UK, a National Literacy Trust reading motivation project which gives children in areas of disadvantage books to choose and keep.

Victoria Carrington is Professor of Education at the University of Plymouth, UK. She writes extensively in the fields of sociology of literacy and education and has a particular interest in the impact of new digital media on literacy practices both in and out of school. Much of what she researches and writes is cross-cut by issues of access and power. She is on the editorial boards of a range of journals and is an editor of the international journal *Discourse: Studies in the Cultural Politics of Education*. Recent publications include co-editing a Special Edition of Discourse: *Studies in the Cultural Politics of Education* on digital literacies with Jackie Marsh (2005); Carrington, V. (2005) 'Txting: The end of civilization (again)', *Cambridge Journal of Education*, Vol 35(2), Summer 2005; Carrington, V. (in press) 'The uncannny, digital texts and literacy' in *Language and Education* and the monograph *New Times: New Families* (2002).

Barbara Comber is a key researcher in the Centre for Studies in Literacy, Policy and Learning Cultures and Professor in the School of Education at the University of South Australia. Her professional passions include pedagogy, critical literacy, social justice and teachers' work. A major professional pleasure is working with radical innovative teacher-researchers. She has recently co-edited three books – *Turn-around Pedagogies: Literacy Interventions for At-risk Students* (with Kamler, 2005); *Look Again: Longitudinal Studies of Children's Literacy Learning* (with Barnett, 2003); and *Negotiating Critical Literacies in Classrooms* (with Simpson, 2001).

Julia Davies is a Lecturer in Education at the University of Sheffield, UK, where she directs the MA in Literacy and Language. Her research predominantly focuses on on-line communities. She has written about teenagers' uses of new technologies to explore issues of identity and the articulation of gender through online formations. She has also focused on changes in literacy and language, looking at ways in which spellings, word choice and emoticons are used to help mark out affinities across individuals with shared interests. She is also looking at the role digital technologies are playing in the development of visual literacies. Julia works with teachers in schools looking at ways in which digital literacies can be embedded more closely into official curricula and is also involved in a school-based longitudinal study, examining gendered patterns of behaviour and achievement of pupils. She has chapters in Marsh and Millard's *Popular Literacies, Childhood and Schooling* (2005) and Buckingham and Willett's *Digital Generations* (2006).

Eve Gregory is Professor of Language and Culture in Education at Goldsmiths, University of London, UK. She has directed projects on family literacy history, siblings and grandparents, particularly in multilingual settings. Her books include *Making Sense of a New World: Learning to Read in a Second Language* (1996), *One Child, Many Worlds: Early Learning in Multicultural Communities* (1997), *City Literacies: Learning to Read Across Generations and Cultures* with Ann Williams (2000), *Many Pathways to Literacy: Early Learning with Siblings, Grandparents,*

Peers and Communities with Susi Long and Dinah Volk (2004) and *On Writing Educational Ethnographies: The Art of Collusion* with Jean Conteh, Chris Kearney and Aura Mor-Somerfeld (2005).

Amanda Hatton co-ordinated the Read Away Derby project for Read On, Write Away! in the UK. Whilst in that role, she conducted a study of the reading practices and experiences of looked after children and young people living in residential children's homes. She is currently a doctoral student at the University of Sheffield.

Jackie Marsh is Reader in Education at the University of Sheffield, UK, where she directs the EdD. Jackie is involved in research that examines the role and nature of popular culture, media and new technologies in early childhood literacy, both in- and out-of-school contexts, and her most recent work in this area was the *Digital Beginnings* project, funded by BBC Worldwide and the Esmée Fairbairn Foundation (see the project website at http://www.digtialbeginnings.shef.ac.uk/). Other recent publications include *Making Literacy Real* (2005, with Larson) and *Popular Literacies, Childhood and Schooling* (2005, co-edited with Millard). She is a founding editor of the *Journal of Early Childhood Literacy* and is currently President of the United Kingdom Literacy Association.

Kate Pahl is a Lecturer in Education at the University of Sheffield, UK. She is Director of the EdD in Literacy and Language in Education. She has written several chapters and articles on the theme of texts and practices in families, and children and popular culture and she is interested in the educational fields of family and community literacy. She is the author of *Transformations: Children's Meaning Making in a Nursery*, (1999) and, with Jennifer Rowsell, *Literacy and Education: The New Literacy Studies in the Classroom* (2005). Her research, funded by the Arts Council of Great Britain via Creative Partnerships, uses ethnography to study the work of visual artists in educational and community settings in the context of regeneration in South Yorkshire. Her edited book, with Jennifer Rowsell, *Travel Notes from the New Literacy Studies: Instances of Practice* (2006) considers the intersection of multimodality and the New Literacy Studies with a collection of ethnographic studies from around the world.

Mark Vicars is a recipient of an ESRC scholarship and was a recent doctoral candidate in the Department of Educational Studies, University of Sheffield, UK. His PhD research used a life-history approach to investigate the formative reading practices and literacy behaviour of gay men. He has published a number of papers which have appeared/are in press in *Sex Education, Auto/Biography* and the *British Educational Research Journal*.

Acknowledgements

We would like to thank warmly all of the authors who contributed to this volume for their excellent contributions and their careful attention to deadlines. Thanks also to Gillian Klein at Trentham for her support of the project from its inception. Finally, we would like to express our gratitude to all of those who attended the United Kingdom Literacy Association's International Conference at the University of Bath in 2005, 'Closing the Gap: Literacy for All'. Your enthusiastic response to, and engagement with, the conference theme confirmed that this book did indeed need to be developed.

1

CLOSING THE GAP

Eve Bearne and Jackie Marsh

This book arose from a UKLA international conference[1], held in 2005, which had as its theme issues of literacy and social inclusion. A number of the chapters are based on presentations given at the conference by keynote and symposium speakers. But this book is not a collection of unrelated conference papers that are connected to a particular theme. Rather, the chapters cohere to present an innovative overview of topics that address questions of literacy, access and social justice. These themes dominated examinations of literacy as a social, cultural and political practice throughout the last century. From Freire's work on raising the *conscientização*, or critical consciousness, of learners in order that they can read the world in addition to the word (Freire and Macedo, 1987:29), to more recent deliberations on the politics of literacy as it is played out in the policies of various nation-states after the legacy of a decade of neo-liberal reforms (Luke, 2004), the emphasis has been on tracing the ideological (Street, 1995) nature of literacy as a social, cultural and economic artefact and practice. The inter-relationship of these various factors are important for, as Rockhill (1994) declared:

> The construction of literacy is embedded in the discursive practices and power relationships of everyday life – it is socially constructed, materially produced, morally regulated, and carries a symbolic significance which cannot be captured by its reduction to any one of these. (Rockhill, 1994, p247)

This book offers specific instances of practice in relation to groups of learners that have traditionally either been excluded from normalised and normalising accounts of literacy education, and/or 'othered' in the process. In doing so, the authors engage with recent debates about the relationship of literacy to notions of social exclusion and inclusion. The various accounts presented focus on particular groups, but they are located within a wider understanding of the nature of literacy education as a heavily politicised process, a process which therefore has specific outcomes for particular groups of learners. In this introduction to the book, we present an overview of the chapters and identify the way in which each chapter relates to the central questions of the text. We begin, however, by exploring what are meant by the terms 'social inclusion' and 'social exclusion' and relate them specifically to literacy education.

Social exclusion

In England, the Social Exclusion Unit was launched in December, 1997, with the aim of recommending policies and strategies to reduce social exclusion. The unit defines social exclusion in the following way:

> Social exclusion happens when people or places suffer from a series of problems such as unemployment, discrimination, poor skills, low incomes, poor housing, high crime, ill health and family breakdown. (Social Exclusion Unit, 2004)

This definition does little to illustrate precisely what social exclusion looks like. Some have suggested that social exclusion results in a lack of participation in civic life, education and employment (Byrne, 1999). Gordon *et al* (2000) suggest that social exclusion is a process, rather than a static state of affairs. It is:

> ...a lack or denial of access to the kinds of social relations, social customs and activities in which the great majority of people in British society engage. In current usage, social exclusion is often regarded as a 'process' rather than a 'state' and this helps in being constructively precise in deciding its relationship to poverty. (Gordon *et al*, 2000, p73).

The term is highly contested, with varying accounts of the nature and causes of social exclusion (Levitas, 2005). However, there is widespread agreement that social exclusion can operate at both individual and community levels. McCrystal, Higgins and Percy (2001) suggested that the factors that contributed to social exclusion at both levels could be identified separately (see Table 1 opposite).

In work on social exclusion, the emphasis has been placed on the integration of the various factors and the effect of multiple indicators in exacerbating the difficulties individuals and communities might face. Poverty has a relationship with social exclusion, therefore, but is not an exclusive factor in its occurrence.

Table 1: Factors associated with the operationalisation of social exclusion

Individual factors

Unemployment
Dependence on state benefit
Debt
Poor health
Low educational achievement
Loss of primary integration

Community factors

High levels of unemployment
Poor local authority services
Poor community resources
Poor housing
Poor public transport
High levels of crime

(McCrystal, Higgins and Percy, 2001)

The term 'social inclusion' has been used to indicate the opposite process to social exclusion, one in which societies aim to ensure that all individuals and communities are included in civic life:

> Social inclusion is the process by which efforts are made to ensure that everyone, regardless of their experiences and circumstances, can achieve their potential in life. To achieve inclusion income and employment are necessary but not sufficient. An inclusive society is also characterised by a striving for reduced inequality, a balance between individuals' rights and duties and increased social cohesion. (Centre for Economic and Social Inclusion, 2002)

The difficulty with such concepts as social inclusion and social exclusion is that they assume a centre of some sort, a society which is cohesive and from which one can be included or excluded through the impact of the factors outlined above. This stark dichotomy between included and excluded can mask a range of inequalities that exist along a continuum in any society. In addition, the narrow interpretation of the concepts by neo-liberal governments means that the focus for policy initiatives is almost entirely on 'back-to-employment' measures. Despite this, the terms have been useful in signalling that the factors that impact upon individuals' life chances are complex and inter-related, rather than focusing only on poverty.

Throughout the chapters in this book, emphasis is placed on highlighting processes that lead to 'literacy exclusion' for some learners and in analysing inclusive practices for literacy education. In the following section, we outline the key concerns relating to literacy and social inclusion and indicate how these issues are addressed in the book.

Literacy and social inclusion

Questions relating to literacy and social inclusion have been the focus for policy-makers in a global context for some years (Unesco, 2006). Levels of literacy are linked to other indicators of social inclusion such as employment and civic participation and therefore the concern of many nation-states has been to ensure that levels of literacy attainment rise in both child and adult populations. In England, there has been a wide range of policy initiatives focused on this area, such as the National Literacy Strategy (DfES, 1998) and Skills for Life (DfES, 2001). In Chapter Two, Viv Bird provides an overview of the policy context within England, an overview that was developed through the National Literacy Trust's 'Literacy and Social Inclusion Project'. Bird's chapter outlines some of the main findings of the Project, a three-year partnership (2002-2005) between the Basic Skills Agency and the National Literacy Trust. The emphasis in Bird's chapter is on the development of strate- gies that are based on strong knowledge of communities and the recognition and valuing of the skills, knowledge and experiences that learners bring to the site of education.

The book then focuses on specific groups and communities in order to ex- plore their experiences in depth. In Chapter Three, Eve Bearne examines issues of gender. For a number of years, the emphasis in many developed countries has been on the apparent underachievement of boys. Since the late 1990s, there have been persistent concerns about boys' achievement in literacy. These concerns have been linked to boys' and girls' different perfor- mances in national tests in reading, writing and English. This approach masks complexities in the situation, however, as 'race' and class impact upon attainment, which means that some groups of girls attain lower results than some groups of boys (Connolly, 2006; Gillborn and Mirza, 2000; Gorard, 2000; Gorard, Rees, Salisbury, 2001). In addition, the move to teacher assessment in the change from Baseline Assessments to the Foundation Stage Profile has resulted in lower results for Black and ethnic minority pupils, a situation which indicates racist assumptions about attainment on the part of some early years teachers (Gillborn, 2005). This under-assessment of pupils from Black and ethnic minority communities has also been identified in cohorts of

4

older pupils (Wilson, Burgess and Briggs, 2006). In addition, the focus on boys has led to a lack of attention to girls' experiences of dissonance between home/school literacy practices (Marsh, 2006). In her chapter, Eve Bearne addresses these complexities in relation to gender, emphasising that boys are not a homogeneous group. She outlines an innovative research project which aimed to motivate boys' writing but which also ensured that girls' needs and interests were addressed. She outlines how engagement in the project was also a powerful form of professional development for the teachers involved and makes a strong case for the place of action research in the search for pedagogies that promote social justice.

As the work of Gillborn and Mirza (2000) indicated, 'race' has a significant impact on educational attainment, although the picture is complicated, with some groups of Black and ethnic minority children out-performing white children. Wilson, Burgess and Briggs (2006) suggest that the causes of under-achievement may be more directly related to community aspirations than other considerations such as poverty, with white, disadvantaged working-class boys appearing to make less progress in secondary education than other ethnic/gender groups, although pupils with Black, African-Caribbean and Pakistani heritage achieve lower scores overall in high stakes examinations taken at sixteen (Wilson, Burgess and Briggs, 2006:1). There is a long tradition of research that has explored the interface between ethnicity and literacy and the work of Eve Gregory has been of central importance in this strand of work. In Chapter Four, Gregory takes a close look at the rich complexity of literacy practices as they occur in family and social groups from different cultures and with a wide range of linguistic repertoires. She examines the wealth of activities that take place in homes and community spaces and the variety of approaches and practices in which families engage and explores the important role played by literacy mediators in children's lives. This analysis presents a strong challenge to deficit accounts of the literacy lives of inner-city children and families and demonstrates the importance of listening and looking closely to the everyday experiences of learners.

This lack of attention to the needs of communities of learners who are normally pushed to the margins of school practice is the case with a group that has received little attention from literacy researchers hitherto, that is, looked after children and young people. In Chapter Five, Amanda Hatton and Jackie Marsh describe a project undertaken by Read On, Write Away! in Derby, England, which aimed to promote engagement in reading by children and young people in public care. They outline how approaches that responded to the interests of looked after children and young people and resisted narrow

5

notions of what 'reading' constituted promoted engagement with, and enthusiasm for, texts. Hatton and Marsh emphasise the need to ensure that looked after children and young people are presented with texts that speak to the realities of their everyday lives.

The importance of encountering texts that enable readers to recognise, explore and celebrate their own identities and practices is the theme of Chapter Six, written by Mark Vicars. Vicars outlines a study in which the reading histories of gay men were explored and argues that the lack of attention to the needs of gay and lesbian learners in educational institutions means that they do not have access to the affirming narratives offered to heterosexual pupils on a daily basis. Drawing from both Queer and reader response theories, Vicars presents an account of transgressive and subversive reading acts that enabled the gay men in his study to explore aspects of their identities in ways denied them in institutionalised settings.

A focus on learner autonomy and agency is also the theme of Chapter Seven, written by Julia Davies and Kate Pahl. They outline the innovative approaches made to curriculum and pedagogy in a College of Further Education (FE). They explore the 'third space' (Bhabha, 1990) engendered when tutors open the walls of the classroom to the interests and experiences of the learners. Paper-based and online material on hip-hop, homelessness and music media ignited the passions of the young learners and allowed them to draw on their everyday literacy practices of texting and MSM-ing.

The dynamic engagement with new technologies that is so evident in the case study outlined by Davies and Pahl was key to the success of that curriculum initiative. In Chapter Eight, Victoria Carrington also considers new technologies, but explores how issues of social inclusion or exclusion are configured in the technological landscapes of contemporary childhoods. Toys, as markers of the specific interests and practices of societies, have been shaped by technological developments for some years, a development which has created controversy and disagreement in the early childhood field over the implications of this for contemporary childhoods (Levin and Rosenquest, 2001; Marsh, 2002). Carrington suggests that the current proliferation of these artefacts, along with representations of children's uses of technology in films and books, indicates that the general perception is now that the ability to access and use such digital technologies is a pathway to social inclusion. She further demonstrates this with an account of 'citizen journalism', outlining how the use of mobile phones, blogs and other technologies to report and reflect on current events enhances the possibilities for community mobilisation and civic participation. Carrington calls for educators to not simply consider issues of access to technologies, but to reflect on uses to which these are put in the classroom if we are to increase opportunities for students' participation and engagement.

Carrington, like other authors in the book, challenges dominant perceptions of the literacy practices of marginalised groups and here, terminology is all-important. Terms such as 'at-risk' do little to counter the deficit model often held of families and individuals by academics and educationalists who equate standard literacy practices with those of white, middle-class communities. In Chapter Nine, Barbara Comber turns this approach on its head by focusing instead on educational approaches which make a difference by acknowledging the rich repertoires of literacy practices communities enjoy. Drawing on Australian projects in which educators engaged with issues of social justice and critical literacy, Comber analyses how teachers committed to socially inclusive practices can draw effectively on these repertoires as they mobilise 'turn-around pedagogies' – pedagogies that make a difference to learners' social and literate identities. This chapter offers a refreshing antidote to the visions of literacy pedagogy that are limited to schooled notions of what it means to be literate and it offers a strong challenge to the limited views of communities living in poverty that are held by many educators. Instead, Comber outlines how work in school can enable learners to do significant and durable identity work, work that makes a significant difference to their life-chances and their orientations to self, school and society.

Conclusion

There are some aspects of literacy and social exclusion/ inclusion that we have not addressed directly. There are many groups and communities marginalised within global education systems and it is beyond the scope of this text to attend to the issues raised with each or all of these groups. The authors in this book look to specific groups in order to explore aspects of research, policy and practice in depth, but identify questions and concerns that are of wider import and that can be applied to all aspects of literacy and social exclusion/inclusion. Overall, the emphasis is not on tinkering with the nuts and bolts of literacy curricula and pedagogy in order that marginalised groups are able to access schooling in a more equal manner, but on addressing more fundamental issues relating to the need to reconceptualise literacy education for the realities of life in the twenty-first century in order that *all* learners can become competent, confident and enthusiastic users and producers of a variety of multimodal texts. If this need is not attended to, then literacy as it is conceived of within schools and colleges is likely to become even more marginal to the lives of children and young people across social, economic and cultural groups thus widening, not closing, the gap between their experiences and educational achievements.

Note

1 UKLA International Conference 'Closing the Gap: Literacy for All', University of Bath, July 7th – 9th, 2005.

2

LITERACY AND SOCIAL INCLUSION: THE POLICY CONTEXT

Viv Bird

Introduction

Social exclusion consists of multi-faceted and interrelated problems, with the cycle of disadvantage now more clearly understood than ever before (Hills and Stewart, 2004). Tackling educational standards, and literacy in particular, has been an important part of the UK Government's strategy to raise economic performance and, since 1997, to address social exclusion. Literacy improvement is often portrayed, particularly in the UK media, as a schools issue. Success or failure is attributed to these institutions alone. Of course, schools play an important role, and we need excellent teachers and well-resourced schools, particularly those which serve disadvantaged and challenging populations. But personal, social and economic circumstances have a major influence on children's motivation and ability to learn and on their literacy skills and educational outcomes.

Families provide the foundations for early literacy development. Parents and other adults support children's language learning through conversation, encouraging imaginative play, and by reading stories, singing nursery rhymes and buying books. They support their children's learning by talking about how they are doing at school, encouraging them to visit the library, and having high aspirations for them to proceed to higher education. When this crucial home literacy support is not there, children start school at a disadvantage and it is more difficult, though not impossible with excellent teaching and robust school support systems, for children to catch up. In economic terms, evidence shows that those with poor literacy are likely to be unskilled, in and out of work and vulnerable to structural changes in the workplace. Recognising the relationship between poor literacy, low self-esteem and low confidence is critical since it is one reason why learners of all ages fail to take advantage of literacy support at different times in their lives. Building confidence is therefore an important element of literacy work with those at risk, working through trusted intermediaries to provide informal learning opportunities in non-threatening locations and encouragement, when appropriate, to participate in further literacy learning.

This chapter is based on the findings of the Literacy and Social Inclusion Project, a three-year partnership (2002-2005) between the Basic Skills Agency and the National Literacy Trust set up to develop an all-age national resource of good practice and 'what works' around literacy and social inclusion. It was concerned with home and community literacy approaches: the under-pinning academic evidence, current literacy practice and the policy frame-work within which practitioners operate. Because the project was not about classroom practice, it did not investigate the processes by which literacy is learned – or taught. Rather, it provided an overview of the evidence base, and the issues and realities faced by practitioners who are trying to engage in literacy learning those of all ages most at risk from their poor literacy skills.

However, there is much common ground with what is known about best classroom practice. Kate Pahl and Jennifer Rowsell (2005) describe the think-ing and application of the New Literacy Studies within primary, secondary and family literacy contexts. They recognise that there are different literacy practices associated with the home, workplace and community, as well as schools, and the importance of drawing on individuals' own experiences and cultural identity to help them access mainstream language and literacy teaching and learning. Pahl and Rowsell highlight the ways that teachers can build bridges between home literacy practices and school learning and, drawing on third space theory, encourage children to 'write out' their home literacy experiences. Where an individual of any age is disengaged from learn-ing or even hostile to formal learning opportunities, the New Literacy Studies provide the pedagogical argument for schools to give greater emphasis to home and community literacy approaches.

Inspection evidence backs this up. Ofsted, the Government agency respon-sible for standards of education in England, found that primary schools that were successful in developing parental support for reading focused on speci-fic initiatives which had involved parents actively reading with their children. General parental involvement is not enough (Ofsted, 2004). Schools need to find out about and build on the reading and writing activities children engage in at home; Ofsted found that primary schools seldom use the broader range of materials pupils use at home as starting points to further their reading in schools and improve their motivation. Such approaches can link formal teaching and out-of-school hours' support with homes and communities and, in the process, help teachers to be more effective.

The Literacy and Social Inclusion Project: Influences and development

The Literacy and Social Inclusion Project was a Basic Skills Agency national support project delivered by the National Literacy Trust. The project developed out of parallel interests of the two organisations[i] which combined the commitment to an evidence-based approach and a vision for how, as a society, we might achieve sustained transformation to improved literacy standards and participation. The vision was articulated by NLT director Neil McClelland (1999):

> I believe that sustained change requires a strategy which contextualises literacy developments within the 'whole picture', by which I mean all those systems issues – social, economic, psychological etc, that work for or against learning, formal and informal. Such a strategy, both across Whitehall and locally, would enable the coherent planning of the jigsaw of interdependent parts that will, if effectively delivered and linked, support a wide range of policy areas including, of course, the National Literacy Strategy.

This means recognising the long-term causal factors which inhibit the transformation of literacy standards, identifying where there is resistance to change and looking for the main influences, within and beyond the education system, which can contribute to the achievement of shared goals. In taking a systems approach to literacy improvement for those most at risk, the Literacy and Social Inclusion Project aimed to bring together collective experiences through a national, largely web-based resource, about what works around literacy and social inclusion. The project looked at policy, research and practice across five key strands:

- promoting early language and literacy
- building parents' skills
- out-of-school-hours literacy support
- motivating disaffected young people
- improving the skills of adults at risk.

The process of data collection (described more fully in Bird, 2005) involved consultations with policymakers and practitioners with wide-ranging professional expertise and policy perspectives. Following an initial examination of the published research evidence, a discussion paper was launched (Bird, 2004), followed by further consultations and a more in-depth look at the research evidence. The questions we asked were: How did research support or extend our understanding of the issues raised, and what were the implications for policy? Our findings and analysis led to an NLT position paper (Bird and Akerman, 2005) which was launched at the University of London Institute of Education at a joint seminar with the National Research and Development Council (NRDC). In focusing on these perspectives, we ensured that the voice of practitioners was heard, reflecting the realities on the ground, but informed by the research evidence. Policymakers benefited from getting a joined-up view even if it meant hearing about the challenges, contradictions and sometimes unintended consequences of well-meant policy decisions.

The policy climate in England

In Chapter One, Eve Bearne and Jackie Marsh explore what is meant by the terms 'social inclusion' and 'social exclusion'. My comments will therefore be brief, aiming merely to contextualise the policy climate as we were developing our evidence base. As John Hills and colleagues from the Centre for the Analysis of Social Exclusion at the London School of Economics acknowledge, social exclusion is a contested term. In England, use of the term began under a Conservative administration when, it was believed, poverty was no excuse for underachievement. The focus on school literacy improvement was continued by the incoming Labour Government in 1997. But it also took on the challenge of poverty and social exclusion in parallel to the drive for higher literacy standards, introducing high-profile targets, national strategies and funding streams to address the 'postcode lottery', so that individuals would not be disadvantaged by the area in which they lived. The Government's definition of social exclusion acknowledged that some people and some communities face a combination of inter-linked problems, for example, unemployment, poor health, low skills, high crime and family breakdown. Others define it as a lack of participation in everyday life: education, community life and active citizenship. Those most at risk of social exclusion include particular groups, such as, Travellers, refugees, children excluded from school or in public care, and the long-term unemployed. Others, too, may be at risk at some stage of their lives such as school leavers without qualifications, or the homeless, also people living in deprived communities, without access to public services. 'At risk' is used here to include people at risk of social exclusion who also have poor literacy or language skills. Developing specific policies with an injection of funding would, it was believed, balance provision more fairly.

The working framework of the Literacy and Social Inclusion Project recognised that these problems exist and need to be addressed for reasons of social justice, economic prosperity and community cohesion. The term 'social inclusion' therefore conveys a positive message that social justice is possible and achievable, given the right conditions for change. So what are those conditions?

Improving literacy is widely recognised as the cornerstone for raising educational standards, encapsulated in the Primary and Secondary National Strategies in England and the Skills for Life national strategy to improve adult literacy and numeracy. In addition, a special Social Exclusion Unit was set up within the Government, and a range of policies introduced which aimed to achieve better outcomes for children, parents and communities. These included: Sure Start, Neighbourhood Renewal, including New Deal for Communities, and Excellence in Cities. Improving the life chances of children is the focus of *Every Child Matters* and its legislative framework the Children Act[ii].

Children's Services have consequently been established, bringing together education and welfare at local government level. Despite huge infrastructural challenges, this presents new opportunities for joint training across professional practice boundaries, provided that childcare targets do not overshadow the need to encourage family literacy support for parents to build their confidence about the importance of their own role in their children's language and literacy learning from the very beginning.

'Extended' or 'community' schools providing extended services such as health and family learning are being actively promoted with Government investment of £680 million. They offer opportunities for literacy partnership approaches that benefit at-risk learners. Alongside the inevitable new directive on how early reading is taught, primary schools should also be thinking about how they are encouraging children to read for pleasure. This means considering how parents and community volunteers can support children's reading development. Secondary schools are judged, understandably, on their place in the published league tables and how many of its pupils attain five good GCSEs; from 2006 these must include English and maths. What impact will this have on the teaching of literacy in secondary schools, through the English curriculum and in other subject areas? Will schools risk experimenting with creative ways of teaching literacy, making explicit links between formal and informal learning, working with community partners in the arts, health, sport and new technology? There is considerable evidence that such approaches, as well as vocational courses, motivate the most disaffected young people, renewing their enthusiasm and self-belief, despite their failure to learn in the past (Golden *et al*, 2004).

The Skills for Life national strategy is suffering a few setbacks, despite having achieved its first milestone of 750,000 new learners. Questions are being asked about whether the strategy is really helping adults with multiple challenges in their lives, including poor literacy. John Bynner's analysis of the Birth Cohort Studies shows that the people most at risk of social exclusion are those with lower level basic skills. Yet there is huge pressure on adult learning institutions to prioritise their resources on provision that leads to the higher Level 2 qualifications (equivalent of good GCSEs). Many believe that this is reducing the capacity of the system to encourage into learning, and retain, the people who most need help. The voluntary and community sector has a key role to play, but the emphasis on courses leading to qualifications makes it more difficult for the sector to attract funding to work with those who are not ready to take national qualifications straight away.

Despite these concerns, there are some indications that these policy initiatives are having a positive effect. With increased spending on education since 1999, evidence shows that progress in schools in the most disadvantaged areas has been faster than elsewhere (Sparkes and Glennister, 2002), although the CASE study highlights tensions between improvements for all and closing the gap (Hills and Stewart, 2004). As a 2005 UK Government Treasury paper acknowledges, 'Securing positive outcomes for all children and young people requires action on a number of fronts reflecting the wide range of factors that influence their lives' (HM Treasury, 2005). The Government remains committed to putting resources into additional support for homes and communities but there is still no national policy directive for an integrated community literacy strategy at local level. What such a strategy would include and the processes involved to get there are considered later in the chapter.

The research link between basic skills and social exclusion
The studies on social exclusion commissioned by the Basic Skills Agency showed clearly that having poor basic skills influences outcomes for adults, especially those at high risk of social exclusion who are also poor readers at the age of 16, think school is a waste of time and want to leave as soon as pos-

sible (Parsons and Bynner, 2002). The same research tells us that poor reading is predictive of adult social exclusion, which is also influenced by social class, level of parental education and whether people live in overcrowded housing. An additional risk factor is having parents with little interest in their children's education or who are unsure about, or do not want them to pursue education or training after the statutory leaving age. The connection between repeated offending and poor basic skills is statistically significant (Parsons, 2002).

In a longitudinal study of twins that used a representative 1994-1995 birth cohort of 5 and 7 year-olds, a strong association was found between reading achievement and antisocial behaviour. For boys, poor reading was associated with behaviour, and vice versa (Trzesniewski *et al*, 2006).

We also know from the research literature that a lack of 'capabilities' leads individuals to become socially excluded. These capabilities are connected to cognitive development and educational success but also relate to an individual's health and whether they play an active part in a community, defined as belonging to a local organisation or faith group, or claiming to vote in elections. We gain capabilities over time – or do not – and they are important in the development of our adult identity, and our ability to getting and sustaining employment (Bynner, 2003). Families play an important part in helping us develop our capabilities. Income (or lack of it), parental education, health (physical and mental) and well-being are all hugely influential. Also important is whether parents involve their children in educational activities, read with them, and take them to arts or cultural events or the library.

A survey commissioned by the UK Government indicates that around one in six adults have low levels of literacy and numeracy but that few adults regard their reading, writing or maths as below average, even those with the lowest levels of ability (DfES, 2003). If people do not recognise their own deficiencies or the potential benefits of taking action it must make the task of persuading them to take up learning opportunities even harder. Other evidence suggests that adults with basic skills needs cannot be easily categorised. Each will have their own experiences and perspectives that will influence their actions. However, the evidence also tells us that they can be helped to see the benefits of improving their skills by means of supportive personal or work relationships (Cieslik and Simpson, 2005).

Numerous studies have investigated the role of motivation. The motivation to read is particularly important since the amount children read for enjoyment is a major contributor to their reading achievement (Clark and Rumbold, 2006). This is backed up by a major international study that showed that reading enjoyment may be more influential on children's success than their family's socio-economic status (OECD, 2003). While motivation is significant, in the social inclusion context, we also need to encourage persistent effort and expectations of success. Changing the deeply held negative views many children, young people and adults have of themselves is a huge challenge and can take a long time (Festinger, 1957). This has implications for how we go about supporting those who are seriously turned off literacy learning.

The evidence points to the importance of informal learning in the community which, for adults, is widely seen to be a trigger for change and development (McGivney, 1999). Some adults, including those with children, will only engage in learning programmes after first getting involved in what is now commonly called 'first steps learning'. Disadvantaged young people with low level literacy also benefit from community approaches which help to build their self-confidence, self-esteem and to learn new skills (Golden *et al*, 2004).

Support for parents

Finding ways to support parents' skills is essential, especially helping them to recognise and encourage the development of their children's language and literacy skills from early infancy. Many studies indicate that what parents do in the home with their children is more influential on later literacy success than social class or parental education (Desforges and Abouchaar, 2003). Children who see adults reading for pleasure are more likely to take it for granted that reading is an important and enjoyable activity and to become intrinsically motivated to read (Clark and Rumbold, 2006). So how do you change parents' behaviours around parenting? There is a great deal of evidence from the US Head Start programmes which were set up to help communities meet the needs of disadvantaged pre-school children. They identified the importance of providing transport, meals, childcare and accessible locations, and encouraging every parent to participate by promoting the programme as a universal service, while targeting high-risk families through home visits and encouragement from parents who have participated earlier.

Evidence from the family literacy demonstration programmes (Brooks *et al*, 1996) reported that attitudes and literacy practices of participating parents improved. These free 12-week programmes were located in areas of multiple deprivation and targeted parents with very low literacy levels. The programmes had three component parts: parents' sessions, children's sessions and joint sessions of parents and children together. Each week, parents were given six hours of basic skills instruction and children six hours of language and literacy support. Parents and children spent an additional two hours together on language and literacy activities.

The strongest evidence of the success of the courses was the huge boost to parents' confidence. Some parents would not have stayed without peer support. It was also noted that programmes avoided an over-concentration on reading, and genuinely focused also on talking and writing. The coordinators emphasised the value to parents of being able to move straight from a session where they learned an activity to do with their children, to a joint session where they could try it out, and, if appropriate, have the parent's role modelled by a teacher. This immediacy delighted the parents as they saw they could help their children. Fathers were found to be less likely to join in family literacy programmes, unless programmes are specifically aimed at them, although their role can be important. Research shows that father and mother involvement at age 7 predicted higher educational achievement by the age of 20 (Flouri and Buchanan, 2001).

Key features of successful literacy and social inclusion work
One thing was clear from all the evidence we examined: we weren't going to discover magic bullets or quick fixes. Finding solutions to help those with personal, social or financial issues in their lives as well as poor literacy, was complex, took time and often required multi-agency support. Yet across the age divide we identified four broad thematic approaches that might lead to literacy improvement:

- engaging individuals and building relationships
- meeting needs and interests
- providing book and reading experiences
- working in partnership and using intermediaries.

Engagement is key. It is best to engage those with low literacy levels and little confidence through activities that do not initially involve reading or writing. You need to start from where they are, and provide interesting and enjoyable learning experiences in settings where they are comfortable. Building relationships with individuals who may be disconnected from their families or marginalised from society helps them connect and gives them a reason to return. The relationship building happens in different ways, between the learner and the teacher, and between learners themselves, and it takes time. It may require home visits to encourage learners to come out of their comfort zone and take a risk. Outreach has to be sensitive. An investigation into community-focused basic skills provision (Hannon *et al*, 2003) highlighted the importance of allowing time for development, that is, the process of engaging people in learning. It is critically important, yet intangible, reflecting the process of developing social capital (Bourdieu, 1986) – individuals report feeling 'more comfortable', they 'enjoy' themselves, they have 'made friends'. What they are doing is building their self-confidence and their personal support networks, in preparation for change in their lives. However, because there are no clear learning outcomes to this process, it is a funding challenge, maybe even a leap of faith, to put in place important building blocks to start the learning process. Time and again, practitioners said to us that engaging learners was what was most needed, and that this was linked to meeting their needs and interests.

It seems obvious that approaches to engage those most at risk from their poor skills need to take account of the interests of particular groups or individuals. Connections may be made with what they know, for example, engaging younger children in discussion and stories around characters they see on TV. The arts, drama and sport motivate people of all ages, as do digital technologies. Family learning is powerful, but initial approaches should focus on practical activities such as making storysacks, so those with low skills levels do not feel excluded. There is a developing evidence base of the success of engaging disadvantaged young people in learning to improve their skills. Accreditation can be motivating, but it may inhibit some young people whose perception of their self-worth is so low that they dare not risk embarking on something at which they might not succeed. Informal learning approaches work best, using a range of materials – newspapers, video, poetry – the arts and sport to link enjoyable activities at the appropriate time with related literacy skills teaching.

None of this is sufficient unless there is a planned focus on literacy, and book and reading experiences are provided. Evaluation of Bookstart, although based on small numbers, has shown the positive benefits of giving books to babies, encouraging families to join the library and involving them in informal rhyme time or story time sessions. Thanks to Government funding, the scheme was extended in 2005 to provide free books for every child at nine months, 18 months and age three. The Peers Early Education Partnership (PEEP), an Oxfordshire-based charity, provides a strong literacy focus in its early learning programme. PEEP works with parents and carers in areas of disadvantage in weekly sessions, using the ORIM framework[iii] developed by the University of Sheffield. Session leaders model different ways of sharing books with children, songs and rhymes are taught, and the contribution of everyday talk is emphasised. Evaluation (Evangelou and Sylva, 2003) showed that children in the PEEP group made significantly greater progress than a comparison group in terms of vocabulary, language comprehension and understanding about books and print, and also showed greater self-esteem. Research has also shown that PEEP supports parents as adult learners, when the parents attend five or more sessions. The social support that the group provided was found to be important. Parents were modelling the techniques they had been shown, looking for words and texts in their daily lives.

It is clear that parenting programmes need to include literacy aims and focus in order to maximise opportunities to develop parents' confidence in talking, singing rhymes and sharing stories with their young children. As parents and carers start to enjoy such activities, their children receive the message that reading is fun and worthwhile. However, poverty means fewer books and computers in the home so schools and communities need to consider how to redress the balance. A survey of school-aged children showed that a greater proportion of pupils not receiving Free School Meals (FSM) had more books in the home than pupils receiving FSM – a recognised indicator of deprivation. They also reported having greater access to resources at home such as a computer or a desk of their own (Clark and Foster, 2005).

The NLT is taking a national lead in encouraging schools to adopt whole-school approaches to reading through its Reading Connects initiative, while Reading Champions celebrates men and boys who are role models for boys to read. The NLT's on-the-ground initiative Reading Is Fundamental, UK(RIF) targets children and young people in areas of disadvantage and motivates them to read by providing free books for them to choose and keep. The Family Reading Campaign is coordinated by the NLT and supported by key partners in the literacy field. It aims to raise awareness of the importance of encouraging families that read, and the need for targeted approaches for parents with poor skills.

Partnership working is a valuable feature of successful approaches to improve the literacy skills of those at risk. Partners might be the library or youth service, culture, sport and health or community-based organisations. Many are already engaged in the literacy improvement or social inclusion agendas, supported by national policy. For example, public libraries support families to develop their children's language, literacy and learning, while many also support adult basic skills activity. The contribution of the cultural agencies and sport is twofold: firstly, they provide interesting local venues which are not stigmatised as 'learning institutions'. Secondly, they offer experiential opportunities that can lead to new engagement with literacy through, for example, creative writing and poetry. The evidence base is patchy, but there are examples of institutions known to be committed to this area of work. Government funding streams such as the National Lottery provide additional funds for the voluntary sector to support literacy learning.

A literacy vision

In our original consultations we found noticeable reluctance among people who were not teachers to intervene to help those with whom they dealt at a professional level improve their literacy skills. This was why *Every which way we can* articulated a literacy vision to encourage professionals across the policy divide – whether working in the education service or the health, housing or criminal justice sectors, to consider their own role in the literacy skills agenda. We need to consider firstly whether it is feasible, secondly, what our own role might be in making the vision a reality and, finally, who we need to persuade to make the current situation change.

The acquisition of good literacy skills is not just an education issue. It is important not to underestimate the challenge and the time it takes to address the personal, social and cultural barriers that prevent many from seeing literacy as something that can be achieved, enjoyed and used productively in their daily lives. There are major policy challenges. Despite increased spending on education over the last nine years, there are still considerable gaps in provision and a shortage of good teachers with the professional and personal qualities to motivate and help those with the greatest challenges. There are still funding barriers, including insufficient money to support the engagement process, which can take time where disaffected young people and adults are concerned. Partnerships are tricky and time-consuming, especially in the important early stages. Some policymakers still need to be persuaded to see literacy as a community issue that cuts across and brings benefits to a wide range of policy areas. A community literacy strategy is proposed that would open up opportunities for partnership working and support schools and others to achieve their targets.

A community literacy strategy

A community literacy strategy (Bird and Akerman, 2005) recognises that we need to support and strengthen families and find ways to improve the literacy skills of groups known to underachieve. This means helping young children to become confident communicators, familiar with rhymes, stories and books and ultimately enthusiastic readers. Parenting support should help parents to play their full part in their child's literacy development in and beyond school. Putting in place a community literacy strategy would help to identify local partners and their strengths. A collaborative literacy process would help all partners to acknowledge that literacy improvement is an inter-professional and intergenerational challenge which, if tackled together, can bring benefits across the board.

This process is illustrated in Figure 2.1:

Figure 2.1: A community literacy strategy

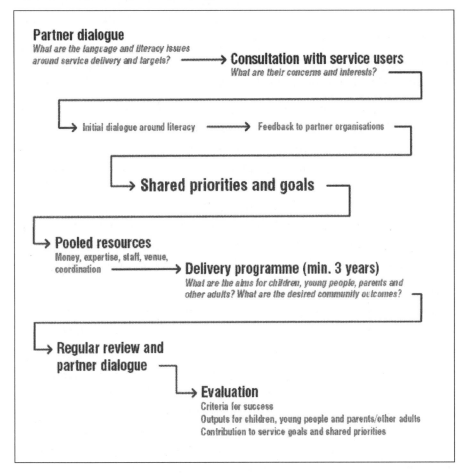

The initial dialogue can take place formally through partnership bodies but also through informal consultations with local organisations. Consultation with service users may highlight barriers to participation, concerns or priori-ties that professionals themselves may not have anticipated or prioritised. By discussing common concerns across the community, shared priorities and goals can be identified. Pooling resources – in the form of money, expertise, staff or venues – can provide a delivery programme to help achieve the desired outcomes for individuals and communities. It can also facilitate risk-taking, test out new approaches to engagement, provide joint training to help professionals work together by sharing their expertise, working practices and knowledge of at-risk groups. This takes time and means that delivery programmes need to be secured for at least three years to enable this collaborative literacy process to develop effective partnerships. It also needs a built-in review and evaluation mechanism so that the delivery programme continues to reflect the needs of all the partners involved and is responsive to the successes and failures of partnership activity.

Starting the collaborative literacy process with different professional groups can be daunting. These are some of the questions which might be considered:

- What priority needs have been identified for children and young people at risk? Is additional literacy support needed?
- Are children and young people encouraged to develop their literacy skills at home? Is this equally true for children and young people in public care?
- Do parenting programmes designed to involve parents in their children's education include a literacy focus? How do they attract, and retain, parents with low level skills, and those not fluent in English?
- Have staff been trained to identify and support clients with literacy needs?

Helping children to develop literacy skills at home includes developing their confidence and pleasure in reading and writing, and encouraging them to use local facilities such as the library.

The intended outcomes need to be agreed by the partners throughout the process. For individuals, the issues may be about confidence and motivation to learn, educational outcomes such as national qualifications, further education or employment. For families, the desired outcomes may be to improve parents' confidence about literacy and their parental skills and to promote more literacy activity in homes and communities and greater expectation of success. For communities, partners may seek improved behaviour, crime reduction and health improvements. Or the priority may be to increase participation in sport and cultural activities like visiting museums and libraries. Another measure may be active community engagement such as volunteering.

Conclusions

The evidence developed by the Literacy and Social Inclusion Project has raised awareness at national level of the steps required for long-term solutions to underachievement. The value of putting community literacy strategies in place has been justified by the evidence. The policy challenge remains, however, and family literacy professionals and others committed to community literacy approaches need to be vigilant, proactively articulating the vision and arguing the case to policymakers at national, regional and local level. The collaborative literacy process will be helped by top-level support, a local coordinator and commitment from community partners.

We have made a start. Let us make sure that, collectively, we put into place strategies that will lead to sustained approaches to support the literacy of those most at risk. Otherwise, there will be serious consequences for social justice, social cohesion, and economic prosperity.

Notes

i The Agency was instrumental in developing the early evidence base around basic skills and social exclusion, working with Professor John Bynner and Samantha Parsons from the Centre for Longitudinal Studies at the Institute of Education, and using cohort study data from the 1958 National Child Development Study and the 1970 British Cohort Study. This work is being taken forward by the National Research and Development Centre for adult literacy and numeracy. The NLT had experience of running the literacy partnerships network which consisted of local authorities working in partnership to strengthen home and community support for literacy, including Read On – Write Away! in Derbyshire. The NLT was instrumental in setting up, in 1996, the Newcastle Literacy Collaborative, a partnership between the NLT and Newcastle City Council which aimed to develop long-term cultural support for the literacy of all who live and work in the community.

ii See glossary (page 24) for an explanation of these policies.

iii Providing Opportunities for learning; showing Recognition of the child's efforts and achievements; Interactions with the child about what they do and feel; and providing a Model of behaviour and actions.

GLOSSARY

The **Basic Skills Agency** is the national agency for literacy, numeracy and related skills for England and Wales (www.basic-skills.co.uk).

Every Child Matters (ECM), and its legislative base the Children Act 2004, provides a national UK framework for improving children's care and life chances. ECM identifies five outcomes needed to improve well-being in childhood and later life: being healthy, staying safe, enjoying and achieving, making a positive contribution, and achieving economic well-being. It is having a major impact on universal services and the education of all children and young people up to the age of 19.

Excellence in Cities is a Government-funded programme introduced in 2000 to provide additional funds to schools for specific approaches to improve exam results and tackle pupil disaffection. By July 2004, the programme covered 1,000 secondary and primary schools in urban areas. It was extended in December 2003 to cover all primaries with more than 35% of pupils on free school meals (a recognised deprivation measure of school populations). These programmes are now locally grouped and known as **Excellence Clusters**.

Extended schools act as a focal point for a range of family and community services such as childcare, health and social services, adult education and family learning, and study support. By 2008, the UK Government intends that at least 1,000 primary schools will have 8am to 6pm wrap-around childcare, and that the majority of schools will be part of a network or partnership providing community services. Schools and teachers are not expected to provide this alone; children's trusts, for example, will play a supporting role.

The **National Literacy Trust** is an independent UK-wide charity which provides a substantial national web-based literacy support network (www.literacytrust.org.uk), runs the Government-funded National Reading Campaign, Talk To Your Baby and on-the-ground initiatives such as Reading Is Fundamental, UK.

Neighbourhood Renewal has been a priority for the UK Government since 2001 with when the Neighbourhood Renewal Unit (NRU) was set up to address common problems in the most deprived neighbourhoods: poor housing, poor health, poor education, few job opportunities and high crime rates. At national level, across government departments, challenging 'floor targets' or public service agreements have been set up concerning education, health, social inclusion, employment and crime. The NRU funds and coordinates a number of initiatives seeking to narrow the gap between the most disadvantaged areas and the rest of the country. Initiatives include New Deal for Communities and the Neighbourhood Renewal Fund.

The **Neighbourhood Renewal Fund** allocates money to deprived communities via area-based multi-agency bodies, known as Local Strategic Partnerships.

New Deal for Communities programmes are characterised by long-term commitment to deliver change, with communities at their heart in partnership with key agencies.

Skills for Life, part of the Government's Skills Strategy, is the national strategy for improving adult literacy and numeracy in England. It includes: a new core curriculum; professional development around new standards for adult literacy and numeracy teachers; reaching out to new learners; and achievement targets for those gaining a national qualification, to increase the numbers of adults with the skills and qualifications needed for economic prosperity.

Sure Start is a UK Government programme which runs in the most deprived regions in England. It aims to achieve better outcomes for children, parents and communities by increasing the availability of childcare for all children, improving health and emotional development for young children, and supporting parents in their parenting role and in their aspirations towards employment. Sure Start has influenced the development of Children's Services, set up as a result of the Children Act (See Every Child Matters above).

3

BOYS (GIRLS) AND LITERACY: TOWARDS AN INCLUSIVE APPROACH TO TEACHING

Eve Bearne

The gender gap has long been a focus for concern in education, particularly in respect of inequities for girls and women. However, national
debates about gender and literacy in many industrialised countries
have recently taken a 'boy turn' (Weaver-Hightower, 2003a)[i]. There is new
emphasis on 'boys' underachievement' (Skelton, 2001) 'lost boys' (Gold, 1995)
and boys 'lapped by girls'(Williams, 1995) in national tests. These themes
have permeated national educational debates in the UK and elsewhere. In
Australia, there has been concern for 'underachieving' and 'under privileged'
boys (Gilbert and Gilbert, 2001; Martino and Berrill, 2003). In the United
States, there have been attempts to make pedagogy more 'boy-friendly'
(Gurian, 2001). Boys are seen both as 'troubled' and as 'trouble' (Titus, 2004)
and in mainland Europe there have been curricular and pedagogic attempts
to develop boys' social and academic achievements (Younger, *et al*, 2005a). In
terms of literacy, the availability of national test data in the UK has identified
a significant gap in attainment between boys and girls, particularly in writing
tests at the end of the primary phase of schooling (DfES, 2005).

Reasons given for this gap in attainment in literacy vary from individual
factors, such as motivation or lack of it (Ofsted, 2003); the absence of strong
male literacy models (Barrs and Pidgeon, 1993); teachers' perceptions of behaviour (Myhill 2000); social constructions of masculinity (Francis, 1998 and
2000; Connell, 1995 and 2000; Rowan *et al*, 2002); teaching approaches (Moss,
2000; Noble and Bradford, 2000); the content of the literacy curriculum

27

(Marsh and Millard, 2000; Marsh, 2003; PNS/UKLA, 2004); and class and ethnicity (Gillborn and Mirza, 2000; Arizpe, 2001). This list alone suggests the variety of competing theories which jostle to explain why boys are scoring less well on formal tests and indicates the complexities of trying to address the issue of boys' underachievement.

Several problems are associated with the debate about 'underachieving boys'. First, there is the definition of underachievement itself and the sense of moral panic which accompanies it (Epstein *et al*, 1998; Martino and Berrill, 2003). Allied to this, the emphasis on boys tends to neglect the position of girls who may be achieving well or, indeed, failing to thrive in literacy. At the same time, there is evidence to suggest that some boys do not present or encounter problems with literacy (Moss 2000; Ofsted 2003; Moss and McDonald 2004; Smith 2004). In many areas of public and educational policy, politicians' pronouncements and media reportage have oversimplified a complex debate (Titus, 2004). Recent research evidence (Younger, *et al*, 2005a) indicates the importance of taking note of the specific nature of every learning situation since community, school and classroom cultures are shifting constructs and the place of boys (and girls) as learners is not static. Also, individual identity is not a given, but varies according to the interactivity of peer, family, popular cultural and community cultural experiences.

The complexities surrounding debates about gender and achievement suggest that in any exploration of boys and literacy it is essential to be clear about just what is under scrutiny. Equally, it is important to make the starting points for any enquiry clear. Different perspectives carry with them specific assumptions and assertions, and rhetoric may not be supported by robust or reliable evidence. Theory about gender difference may not work hand-in-hand with school and classroom practice (Weaver-Hightower, 2003a).

However boys' achievements are described or theorised, it has to be acknowledged that test scores have consequences for learners. In terms of pupils' futures, low attainment has potentially significant implications for access to further and higher education and for job prospects, and so demands attention. Whilst the reasons for boys' lower test scores are complex and varied, influenced by factors out of school as well as within the classroom, the gap in attainment needs to be taken seriously. From the schools' point of view, although a sceptic might point to an investment in raising test scores because of league tables of results, initiatives aimed at tackling the gap in attainment between boys and girls are generally prompted by a genuine desire to help learners achieve their potential. Many teachers are professionally and personally troubled by the sense that some learners just aren't engaged in learning. With these matters as a background I want to look at a research and intervention project carried out by the United Kingdom Literacy Association (UKLA) in collaboration with the Primary National Strategy (PNS) in England in 2004.

Raising Boys' Achievements in Writing research project

In 2003 the Primary National Strategy identified boys' achievements in writing as a key issue and the *Raising Boys' Achievements in Writing* research project was intended to tackle differences in attainment. Although focusing on boys, the research acknowledged from the outset that there are differences *between* boys as well as between boys and girls. The focus was firmly on pedagogy aimed to develop effective teaching approaches which would specifically address boys' achievements whilst offering a sound teaching model appropriate to all learners. It began with the assumption that any underachievement is a proper concern for everyone involved in education – parents, teachers and children – but that it is wise not to take on generalised views about boys, girls and writing without asking a few questions or gathering first-hand information before starting specific activities. Careful observation and monitoring were seen as essential so that teaching approaches could be developed to support boys' (and girls') achievements.

Teacher research groups of eight to ten teachers each in three different areas of the UK: Medway, Essex and Birmingham, worked over two terms on teaching units designed to raise boys' engagement, motivation and achievements in writing, using either visual stimuli including integrated technologies or drama activities (UKLA/PNS 2004). The term 'integrated technologies' denoted the use of visual stimuli generated by different digital technologies: video and DVD and the associated use of remote control devices and computer texts of all kinds, alongside the more traditional 'technologies' of writing, model making, artwork and puppetry. The teachers involved were all Leading Teachers[ii] or were identified by their local authority as expert practitioners. Each selected a focus group of five or six boys whom they felt were not achieving as well as they might (including those who were potentially high achievers) and kept writing samples and assessments as well as observations and their own reflections over the period of the project. The classes involved ranged from early years to the end of primary phase schooling.

The emphasis on visual approaches to teaching and learning was prompted by a concern that although there are many passing references to boys' visual preferences in learning (Maynard, 2002; Noble and Bradford, 2000) there has been little research specifically designed to probe the link between the visual and boys' writing. Key British researchers into boys' literacy (Millard 1997; Moss, 2000) have identified the importance of the visual and this has been echoed by reports from the inspectorate (Ofsted, 2003) and DfES funded research (Warrington and Younger, 2006). Some recent work has examined the relationship between visual and audio-visual texts and writing (Higgins, 2002; Parker, 2002; Essex Writing Project, 2002 and 2003). There is also increasing awareness of the centrality of visual texts in the literacy curriculum as a whole (Kress, 1997; Bearne, 2003). The collaborative PNS/UKLA research offered a source of systematically gathered data about the relationship between visual stimuli of various kinds (still image, moving image, artefacts, multimodal books) and the development of boys' writing.

The high profile of drama in the project was based on rather more substantial evidence. Research examining the effect of drama on writing concludes that drama and writing have a complementary, interactive and mutually reinforcing relationship (Neelands, 1993) and that role play and other drama conventions make a much more effective contribution to writing than just discussion (Booth and Neelands,1998; Wagner, 1994). McNaughton (1997) notes that children who engage in drama before writing write more effectively and at greater length than those who engage only in discussion. Process drama supports learners as they generate ideas, adopt alternative stances and roles and engage imaginatively. As Grainger argues, the symbolic and transformative nature of drama appears to increase the relevance and purpose of writing and enables writers to focus and write with greater fluency, energy and voice (Grainger *et al*, 2005).

There are potential disadvantages to a relatively short-span (six months or so) project: shifts in performance in writing and other factors such as motivation, attitudes and changes in writing behaviours may not be easily observable in a few months' work. However, previous experience of similar short projects from the DfES (Younger *et al*, 2005a) and Essex projects (2002 and 2003) suggested that there would be useful evidence to support the value of the teaching approaches being used. It was also important to ensure comparability across the three areas working on the project because of possible differences arising from the focus on drama or integrated technologies. As the work progressed, however, this became less of a concern since the teachers often combined both approaches.

In aiming for generalisable evidence across the three projects, different types of data were collected and analysed:

- survey data on children's perceptions about themselves as writers
- samples of children's writing and teachers' assessments and commentaries
- contextual information about the schools, classes and pupils involved
- teacher observations and evaluations.

Pupil perceptions surveys were repeated at the end of the project and writing samples analysed using national assessments and content analysis. Teachers' reflective observations provided data for evaluations of the teaching model. The sample as a whole comprised 105 pupils in nineteen classes (seven in Birmingham; six from Essex and six from Medway) representing classes of four year-olds through to eleven year-olds with 28 teachers involved in the project.

Teacher meetings were held to help the teachers involved to see their work as part of a national initiative and to share examples of good practice. An initial launch meeting also provided sessions about drama and visual approaches to literacy which were followed up with some supplementary activities in local areas.

Planning and carrying out units of work

Before any of the teaching units were planned, the teachers surveyed pupils' perceptions about writing. The initial perceptions survey (see Appendix) had a dual purpose, designed not only to provide baseline data but also to give the teachers information to help them plan their classroom work. The survey data provided teachers with a snapshot of their focus group boys' perceptions in three main areas:

- attitudes to writing and views of themselves as writers (questions one to four)
- preferences for specific types of writing (questions five to seven)
- out-of-school writing practices and experiences (questions eight to ten).

Questions one to four were intended to provide some baseline data against which shifts in perceptions could be measured and were repeated at the end of the project. Questions five to ten were used to inform teachers about their focus group boys' writing preferences and their experiences of writing at school and at home. The teachers themselves analysed these responses.

All the teachers found the surveys informative and useful but some were surprised when their boys responded with unexpectedly negative views of writing. They were particularly concerned about the number of boys who seemed to think that 'writing' was restricted to spelling and handwriting. This allowed discussion of the point that pupils will often make apparently restricted or negative comments because they do not have a vocabulary for talking about writing. If at the end of the project there was evidence of a more extensive use of metalanguage, this would suggest pupils' more secure grasp of concepts about writing.

The analysis of the pre-project surveys highlighted several recurrent themes in the responses, for example, the number of boys who remembered success-ful pieces of their writing from several years before the survey, who habitually write and draw at home although they do not write readily at school and who mentioned parents and family members writing at home. The teachers were also struck by the number of boys who indicated that they wanted greater choice, for example, of topics for writing and who mentioned the importance of security factors: working with friends, having teacher approval or being sure about what the task required. These observations were common across all year groups and areas.

With these insights to guide their thinking, the teachers began to plan for their first extended unit of work. The general pattern would be to immerse the pupils in the text type they were studying, explore its features through film, drama, artwork and ICT, then in the final stages of the unit move towards the pupils producing a piece of writing which they had time to work on and improve to their own satisfaction. This might be handwritten, presented as a book, or on screen.

The teachers had varying levels of experience in using integrated tech-nologies and drama to support writing but they entered into the work en-thusiastically. Many used DVDs of films which had been on general release, including different versions of the Peter Pan story or animated popular films such as *Finding Nemo, Monsters Inc., Pocahontas* and *Shrek* while a few based their work on epics such as *Lord of the Rings.* Other teachers used a range of drama techniques to develop themes found in picturebooks, novels, poetry or films. As the work progressed, and as teachers started on their second ex-tended unit of work, many used a combination of integrated technologies and drama to support the development of writing.

Two brief case studies give a flavour of the work.

Ruth Wells, who took a drama focus, taught a class of eight- and nine-year-olds in large junior school in an urban overspill area of Kent. Pupils come from mixed socio-economic backgrounds, and the proportion of children with special needs is in line with the national average. The class of 27 pupils had some highly achieving girls but the boys were described as of average or below average achievement. She noted:

> The boys were selected because of their lack of achievement and progress in writing, in both literacy and other subjects, regardless of their National Curriculum level. Most lacked motivation and would find displacement activities rather than write. Strong factors against writing included: *making your hand ache*, worries about poor spelling and presentation and *being told what to write about.*
>
> One of her three week units was designed to fit with the recommended text type for the age group: Multicultural Texts. *Mufaro's Beautiful Daughters* by J. Steptoe was selected not only because it is a text based in Africa but also because it raised issues and dilemmas for the characters involved, and drama readily lends itself to the exploration of relationships, conflict and resolution. The work began with the class using Freeze Frames to represent their predictions about how the story would end, drawing on their prior knowledge of the text type. Other drama activities during the work included Hot Seating, Role on the Wall, Overheard Conversation, Decision Alley and Group Sculpture, as well as circle time where the class discussed issues and the characters' emotions and behaviour. The drama activities culminated in a wedding ceremony. By this stage in the work, the class were taking control of the drama, becoming more independent of my input and, in fact, inviting me to take part as a photographer.
>
> By the end of the unit the boys' attitudes to enjoying writing had moved forward. Although they were still anxious about their secretarial skills, one boy found that he needed to use more interesting vocabulary (although he said that it 'gives me harder spellings what I can't spell'). More importantly, his reason for definitely enjoying writing now was because, '... it puts good memories in my head'. Writing was less physically demanding than previously, and the drama work that had been lived in order for the writing to happen allowed them to write for the meaning they wanted to convey.

In Essex, Heather Hann used visual approaches for one of her three-week units with a class of ten- and eleven-year-olds in a mixed catchment suburban school. In this class the boy/girl ratio was evenly balanced. In writing, however, there was a heavier bias towards boys who were not achieving their full potential. Heather writes:

> The class were due to cover the recommended themes for the year group: *changing narrative structures and fantasy stories.* The use of dialogue, describing action and structuring narrative through paragraphing were also key

issues the pupils needed to work on. Embedding ICT in literacy was also a key priority and the genre of fantasy offered the opportunity to use puppets and the digital cameras to produce extended narratives.

Pupils watched DVDs to identify the impact of camera angles on the reader and understand how they could use the idea of point of view in their writing. They then took still images of key aspects in the story with digital cameras, using their awareness of camera angles to tell the narrative from a chosen perspective.

By using integrated technologies, the pupils saw themselves as directors of the images and narrative. They were familiar with presentational software but had not used it as a creative tool before. The digital still images were put into the software to generate the narrative.

There were several ways in which the work affected the writers:

- The quality of discussions between the pupils and their change in attitude towards writing were very noticeable.

- There was good progress overall, especially in attitude and self esteem as writers.

- Pupils became 'directors of their words' rather than writers.

- Use of paragraphs in writing improved.

- Dialogue was used by the pupils to move the narrative along.

- An unexpected element was the improvement in joined and fluent handwriting.

- Pupils began to use connectives at the beginning of sentences in order to indicate shifts of time and place.

But perhaps most important of all was the fact that pupils talked about the work outside the classroom and walked taller as writers.

These two brief glimpses show activities which involve audio-visual, gestural and dramatic texts as well as a great deal of discussion and pupil involvement. In these two cases, as in the others, the pupils took greater charge of their own work. The 'directorial eye' drawn from drama experience or from being in charge of taking photographs, fed into their writing, so that pupils showed a greater sense of audience awareness and control of their narratives. In addition, the lived drama experiences and the discussions surrounding choices of image meant that these young writers felt they had something to say. As a result, the young writers found greater satisfaction in writing.

The teachers also found greater satisfaction in using a planning structure which allowed them to work more flexibly and creatively, prompting them to listen to the children more carefully in the process, responding to their needs and ideas. When the teachers evaluated their work they agreed on some key factors which had contributed to the pupils' successes: they had planned work according to the insights from the pupil perception surveys, designing activities to suit the pupils' diverse experience – of texts and of life. They had also slowed the pace of learning, providing greater space for reflection, allowing pupils more time to talk before writing and more choices about how to record their work. They had also been far more explicit about the ways different texts are constructed. Reflections on the project had implications for a more inclusive pedagogy.

Progress: The writers and their attitudes to writing

The comparative analysis of pre- and post-project pupil surveys indicated significant gains made in attitudes to writing and to the boys' perceptions of themselves as writers. At the start of the project, the focus groups of boys reported a range of negative factors about writing. These were often related to frustrations about technical accuracy but were also linked with physical tension, time pressure, lack of ideas or emotional factors related to anxiety. After the project, negative comments were reduced by half and indications of anxiety and physical tension were almost entirely eradicated.

One question: *What advice would you give to a younger reader to help them improve their writing?* was designed to probe the boys' available meta-language about writing before and after the project. Pre-project responses were again largely related to technical features and 'good behaviour'. After the project there was a noticeably wider range of comments. There were still a good number advising on technical features, but there was more assurance about taking care over work and a clear sense of the whole process of getting and communicating ideas through talk, drama, visual and media texts. Overall, the boys seemed to have grasped a fuller sense of how writing is a matter of communicating ideas, getting your own ideas across, rather than the predominant earlier view of writing as a technical exercise.

After the project, Chris (aged five) had more to say about improving writing (scribed comments):

Pre-project: *I'd say watch me I'm a good writer because I think about words.*

Post-project: *You need to think about your setting and your characters – choose some good characters and some bad characters and make it interesting by thinking what they might do.*

Jemal (aged seven) showed a distinct flavour of self-improvement after the project:

Pre-project: *Draw pictures and copy sentences.*

Post-project: *If you write more you will improve and be able to read your work to the class. Use videos and DVDs to get ideas from.*

At nine years of age, Osmur had certainly got to grips with grammatical terminology but after the project he showed a sense of the importance of writing for communication:

Pre-project: *Openers, connectives, verbs, adverbs, time connectives, words for said, handwriting.*

Post-project: *Keep on trying, writing at home, listening and talking of your ideas.*

As might be expected, with older pupils there was greater emphasis on whole text structure, but Owen (aged eleven) came to see himself as a writer who could gain satisfaction from writing:

Pre-project: *Have a very good opening and good middle and a good way to finish off what has just happened for the end.*

Post-project: *Always remember your punctuation, try your best at spelling, use paragraphs, neat handwriting and most of all just try your best. Enjoy it.*

Progress: The teachers' observations

The teachers' observations on the boys' attitudes to writing emphasised their enhanced independence, enthusiasm, confidence and motivation. In addition, they noted improvements in reading and, more strikingly, in speaking and listening. Overall, the teachers continually commented on the boys' greater pride in themselves and their work, their increased belief in their own ability and a sense of feeling valued. Physical signs of these changes were evident in the boys' body language, with the teachers reporting less fidgeting or 'lolling' and generally more alert posture. There was a strong sense that the boys were far more ready to be adventurous in their ideas and to take risks with the technical features of writing.

A key feature of improvement throughout the age range was the boys' readiness to sustain commitment to a chosen piece of writing. The teachers noted that the boys remained on task for long (or longer) periods of time, seeing work through to the end. They were also more prepared to check work, review and improve it and generally seemed more in control of the process of their writing. Markers of greater independence were: settling more readily to tasks and not needing reminders from the teacher; working more harmoniously with others; being prepared to make mistakes and learn from them and relishing making choices about what and how to write. They were developing identities as writers.

Perhaps the most reported area of improvement in the writers' attitudes was in their enthusiasm, confidence and motivation, indicated by wanting to write and volunteering to take part in discussion, to ask questions and to advance ideas. Their increased assurance to talk about their own writing and to articulate feelings in front of others were equally striking. The boys showed a greater sense of being part of a learning community, as evidenced by readiness to share work with others and to bring work from home to show to the class, so enhancing a sense of community.

Evaluating the project

Evaluation by the teachers, PNS colleagues and the researchers themselves indicated markedly successful project outcomes. The model which combined an extended approach to teaching with specific attention to drama and/or integrated technology proved highly successful in raising boys' achievements in writing. There were also significant gains in the teachers' professional development and sense of personal and professional satisfaction. Also, although the focus was on underachieving boys, the work had beneficial effects on other pupils' – both boys' and girls' – writing and attitudes to themselves as writers. Using drama and visual approaches in teaching had resulted in marked and rapid improvements in the focus group boys' writing, with over 70% exceeding the rate of progress which might be expected.

It would be easy to use the evidence as a vindication of the increasingly fashionable notion of 'learning styles' and particularly those which stress the visual, auditory and kinaesthetic (VAK). It could be argued that since visual and the kinaesthetic featured highly in the project work this focus accounted for the improvements in perceptions, performance and increased feelings of self-worth amongst the boys involved. However, the picture is rather more complicated than might at first appear. The improvements made by the pupils involved in this project did not come about by simple application of a visual, auditory and/or kinaesthetic approach to learning. Indeed, recent research in schools which have adopted a deliberately 'kinaesthetic' approach to teaching indicates no conclusive evidence to support such claims (Younger *et al*, 2005b). There are dangers in apparently 'simple solutions to complex problems' (Coffield *et al*, 2004:210) and this project indicates greater complexity than a simple 'learning styles' approach.

A more fruitful means of understanding what contributed to the success of the work lies in theories of multimodality (Kress, 2003; Bearne, 2003). Evidence from the UKLA/PNS project suggests that adopting an integrated approach where sound, gesture, image and written (or symbolic) systems work together is more likely to provide a learning context which is inclusive and accessible. The teachers' planning showed how an integrated, holistic approach to teaching writing can support diversity and choice – both diversity in the pupils' learning preferences and diversity of their text experience. This was reflected in the fact that almost all of the pupils made gains in their writing, not just the focus group boys. As Marsh argues in her work on gender and popular cultural texts (Marsh, 2002), it is important to adopt inclusive practices which 'reflect the needs and interests of *all* children in today's society' (Marsh, 2003: 79).

At the same time, adopting a teaching approach to literacy which extended the repertoire to include making and responding to drama, visual and ICT texts afforded greater scope for explicit examination of differences in the texts used. The teachers found themselves paying more conscious and deliberate attention to the ways in which texts work to make meaning, discussing how gesture represents what might be written, how sound might be captured in words, or when words might be entirely unnecessary in expressing meaning. They developed a professional vocabulary of multimodality as they expanded their own expertise.

Most important of all, perhaps, was the teachers' acknowledgment of the experience, or 'funds of knowledge' (Moll *et al*, 1992) learners bring from their worlds outside school. They listened to the children talk about films, comics, computer games, or about their feelings and experiences of an emotional world outside the classroom which they explored and expressed in drama work. The pupils brought a range of experience to the classroom drawn from their home cultural knowledge of texts and their experience of life itself. What the project provided was a means through which knowledge and experience of this kind could be given space and the pupils a voice. Boys who had been described as underachieving in writing began to see themselves as successful and satisfied writers. There are, as I have observed, considerable problems associated with the whole notion of underachievement. Also, in evaluating this project there has not been a chance to assess whether the gains made by the young writers have been maintained. Nevertheless, the successes of this project strongly suggest the value of a multimodal teaching approach which values and draws on children's diversity and their knowledge of texts and experiences in their lives outside the classroom. In seeking to close some of the gaps – in attainment or between home and school literacy practices – a curriculum based on principles of multimodality and diversity is more likely to answer to the needs of all learners, rather than just 'underachieving boys'.

Notes

i While acknowledging that the 'boy turn' in gender debates in now an international issue in industrialised countries, for the remainder of this chapter I focus on the UK.

ii Leading Teachers are practising classroom teachers/practitioners who have been identified by their Local Authorities as having exemplary practice. They support the work of the Local Authority in professional development with other teachers.

Appendix

Writing perceptions survey

You may need to adapt the questions for the younger classes, and decide whether you want to ask your class/focus group to fill this in as a questionnaire or respond orally.

- Do you enjoy writing? Why? / Why not?

- Is there anything you don't like about writing? (This may have been covered by responses to the above)

- Are you a good writer?

- Is there any particular kind of writing you enjoy more than others?

- Can you remember a piece of writing you did when you were younger that you were particularly proud of? Why was that?

- What's the best piece of writing you've done recently? What was good about it?

- Do you ever write at home for your own pleasure? What?

- Do you ever draw at home? (This may be helpful for younger children)

- Does anyone else write or draw at home?

- What advice would you give to someone in the year below you to help them get better at writing?

4

WHAT COUNTS AS READING AND LEARNING OUTSIDE SCHOOL? AND WITH WHOM? HOW? AND WHERE?

Eve Gregory

Nicole, aged five, was born in England but moved with her parents and grandparents when she was two to live in a small village in Normandy, France. By now, she is bilingual, speaking French at school and to her friends in the village, English to her parents, grandparents and pets. She is also an emerging biliterate, learning through phonics and sound clusters in French with her class at school, prediction and repetition of words and rhymes in English with her mother at home. On this occasion, I give her an unusual book 'The A to Z Gastronomique' (Sharman and Chadwick 1989) which alphabetically lists French food (in French) and provides a short description beside it in English. Sometimes, a picture is provided. Nicole turns to the page where she sees a picture of a fish called 'colin' (French for hake) and the following text:

COLIN *(which she pronounces 'kôlé')*

Hake, also known as saumon blanc, merlu, merlan and canapé....'

As usual, she sounds out the word in French. Then she turns to the picture and looks puzzled, since the word, pronounced in French, has no meaning for her. After a few further attempts with the French pronunciation, a sudden look of enlightenment comes over her face: 'Oh, I know! It's Colin (pronounced as in the English name) the Cod, isn't it?' Colin the Cod was a character in one of her English TV cartoons.

F or Nicole, understanding the meaning of the text counted as much towards reading (at least at home) as 'getting it right' in terms of pronouncing the word correctly. It all depended on the context in which she found herself. On another occasion, Nicole gave her personal view on the differences between reading in French and in English, '*When you read in French, your lips come out like this (she purses her lips into an 'ü') and when you read in English, they don't*'. Nicole is lucky. As a mother-tongue speaker of a prestigious language, her home interpretation of what 'counts' as reading is valued by her teachers in school. She is often asked to demonstrate her English and her mother is invited to impart her language skills to groups of children; sessions they regard as an important privilege.

Her peers living in East London, England, are not so lucky. They also have very different interpretations of what counts as reading outside school, but their teachers remain largely unaware of and thus exclude their home practices and corresponding languages. Louthfur is also aged five and, like most of his peers living in Spitalfields, East London, he attends both Bengali and Qur'anic classes. At Qur'anic class, he learns to read the Qur'an in classical Arabic:

> The class takes place in a neighbour's front room. About thirty children of all ages including Louthfur line the walls like a human square, seated with their raiel (a beautifully carved wooden stand upon which to place the Qur'an or the initial primers) in front of them. There is a loud hum as they all chant their individual practice piece... Like many of the children, he (Louthfur) rocks to and fro to the sound of the voices. Children do this because they are encouraged to develop an harmonious voice; they are told Allah listens to his servants and is pleased if time is taken to make the verse sound meaningful. (Gregory, 1996, p41)

Louthfur cannot understand the meaning of the words he is reading in classical Arabic. Yet it is clear that what 'counts' is pronouncing the text beautifully. There will be another occasion when a teacher can explain to him the meaning of what is being read. In contrast with Nicole, however, there is no recognition at school of either his Qur'anic or Bengali knowledge. The learning style of both classes contrasts with that of his English class, where he faces questioning and comprehension exercises on the meaning of words and sentences he has just read.

The second half of the 20th century and the early 21st have seen increasing recognition in Britain of the role of the family in children's literacy achievement. This has been reflected in a number of government reports informing

Figure 4.1: Changes in what 'counts' as appropriate home reading activities from the end of the 20th to the beginning of the 21st centuries

us what the 'good' or 'enabling' family environment looked like (DES, 1967, 1975, 1988, 1996; Ofsted, 1996). The role of the family has similarly been the focus of various research studies showing the cognitive and linguistic advantages accrued by children profiting from 'appropriate' home activities (Bernstein 1973; Hewison and Tizard 1980; Wells 1987). During the 1970s and 1980s, 'enabling' parents were those sharing the story-reading practice by reading stories aloud (usually at bed-time) to their children; by the beginning of the 21st century, parents were being encouraged to purchase 'Jolly Phonics' materials (Lloyd, 2004) and to find out about the latest advantages of synthetic phonics reading schemes.

Whatever approach has been suggested, however, there has always been one particular way that 'counted' as 'right' at the time. Families whose literacy practices fell outside this frame tended to remain invisible in both government reports and research studies.

However, a growing number of ethnographic studies taking place in the homes of ordinary families in both the US and the UK at the end of the 20th century began to reveal widespread and complex different literacy practices, indicating that families from all cultural and social groups had long participated in a variety of literacy activities which were just as effective as the 'official' literacy that counted at school (Heath 1983; Taylor and Dorsey-Gaines 1988; Moll *et al*, 1992; Gregory 1996; Volk 1999; Gregory and Williams 2000; Hull and Schultz 2002).This chapter provides examples that fall within the above tradition. It argues for a model of *contrasting but complementary literacies* whereby children benefit from home literacy practices that are very different from those counting at school. The first part of this chapter investigates the nature of 'invisible literacies' by highlighting the remarkable linguistic, cognitive and cultural flexibility shown by young children living in London's East End before World War Two. Using reminiscences of people born during the early part of the 20th century (mostly the Jewish community) it unpicks the *wealth of activities*, the *variety of methods* and the *number and type of literacy mediators* in children's lives.

The second part of the chapter investigates further the role of different and usually 'invisible' mediators of literacy in young children's lives more than half a century later. However different the approaches officially suggested over the last century, *all* assumed reading to take place only between caregiver (generally the mother) and child. This chapter reveals young children as active members of wider family groups and illustrates particularly the interaction between siblings and grandparents and young children as they work and play together during literacy activities. It thus argues that the early years of the 21st century begin to reveal a paradigm shift from a focus on the dyadic relationship between parent as expert and the child as novice towards viewing the child as a skilled member of complex family and social groupings, participating in different literacies according to the people involved and the context in hand.

Invisible literacies in the lives of two generations in London's East End

> I remember going to the library, and in those days, you could go by yourself. I went on my own. I remember, it used to be dark. I suppose it was the middle of the winter. Pitch black... I found a release in books... I still remember the books I read because they were so different from my everyday life... There was one particular girl who went right through all this series of books and I couldn't wait to get the next book... (Norma, born in 1929, in Gregory and Williams, 2000, p88-89)

The people in this section all recount their memories of home and community reading as they grew up in London's East End. The area of Spitalfields where they lived is just east of the City and has a long history of receiving immigrants; the Huguenots during the eighteenth century, followed by Jews from Eastern Europe during the latter half of the nineteenth and early 20th centuries. In this section, I begin to reveal their reading practices by investigating the wealth of activities in which they engaged, the variety of methods and approaches used as they set about learning and the number and type of mediators involved in helping them to become members of different reading groups.

Minnie, Abby, Aumie, Norma, Gloria and Stanley all grew up in and around Spitalfields during the early part of the 20th century. By its close, Minnie, the eldest, was ninety, Abby and Stanley in their eighties, Norma and Aumie in their seventies and Gloria, the youngest was sixty-one. All except Stanley were born into Jewish households. Immense social changes had taken place even between the time that Minnie, the eldest, and Gloria, the youngest, were growing up. Minnie, Stanley and Abby started school barely half a century after huge tracts of land had been torn up for the railway lines which were to divide east London, less than thirty years after Jack the Ripper had terrorised his victims just a stone's throw from where they were to live and less than twenty years after animals were driven into open slaughter houses in Aldgate. When Minnie, Abby and Stanley began school, horse-drawn buses, bicycles and hand-carts all streamed down the Whitechapel Road into the City of London. By the time that Gloria was leaving primary school, both Spitalfields and the City were peppered with bomb-sites, horse-drawn buses had been replaced by trolleys and planes and cars had replaced the railways as symbolising progress – but only for the rich. Like most of their East End peers, none of the children were able to continue their formal education beyond fourteen. Their informal learning, especially literacy learning, was a different matter.

The wealth of activities, methods and mediators of literacy in the lives of older East Enders

In spite of considerable economic poverty, there existed a wealth of literacy practices in the lives of older East Enders, who spoke of elocution lessons and speech choirs, recitation, reading the classics, newspapers and comics, visiting the theatre, learning Hebrew and attending out-of-school English literacy classes, amongst numerous other activities (Gregory and Williams, 2000, 86-87). Minnie, for example, travelled four miles by bus for her weekly class:

Minnie: ... and I continued that English literacy class until we moved to Forest Gate. My mother didn't like me going there on the bus because, even in those days, the cost was fourpence for me.

AW: And what did you do there?

Minnie: All sorts of things. Mrs. Henriques used to read to us and teach us... she read English, all English. Some were very poor. They used to run there from school because their mothers went to work and they'd come about seven o'clock and some of my friends got to the top... very able... they couldn't even afford fourpence for the gas mantle... A lot of the boys learned to read. And Mrs. Henriques used to say, 'It is a very important thing.' (Gregory and Williams 2000, p88)

Aumie remembered both his library books in English, where he loved everything about public schools, cricket and rugby, and his Hebrew classes which left a deep impact on him:

We would go five times a week. So you'd come home from school... and then by five o'clock, we would be in Hebrew classes until 7, and, as far as I was concerned, by 8 o'clock, I was back in the choir for rehearsals twice a week ... (Gregory and Williams 2000, p89)

The methods by which they learned were extremely varied, although none corresponded with the reading aloud approach of the Bedtime Story routine that was to prevail later in the century. Interestingly, all remembered clearly the methods by which they felt they learned. Although Abby's memories below are from school, she also practised a lot at home:

Abby: We used to do everything by rote. It would be put up on the board and we would repeat what the teacher said. 'Cat', 'Dog', that kind of thing...

EG: Can you remember if you learned it by the sounds, like 'k' 'a' 't' [sounds it out] or did you learn the whole word 'cat'?

Abby: 'Cat' [the whole word]. You might have learned the letter sounds as well, like 'k' 'a' 't' and that sort of thing, but it was the whole word and you repeated it by rote. Mostly, you said the letter names 'c', 'a', 't'. You didn't pronounce it 'k' 'a' 't' [sounding it out] the way schools do now. And we used to have chalk slates... (Gregory and Williams 2000, p91)

Aumie, on the other hand, remembered learning both phonics and grammar at his Hebrew classes:

You would learn phonetically, the twenty-four letters of the Hebrew alphabet... We would learn letter by letter and then build up the words... Learning Hebrew phonetically like this we were soon able to learn quite quickly. We would read mechanically without understanding the words... at the age of 7, we were learning Hebrew grammar, which is far more complicated in many ways than English grammar, so when we were in the English school, adjectives, nouns and verbs, things that our non-Jewish friends were just beginning to grapple with, were all very natural to us. (Gregory and Williams 2000, p91)

By the time Gloria started school, towards the end of World War 2, new methods in the teaching of reading were being tried out:

I remember coming home with this book, this Phonoscript First Primer, and sitting down, not very often, but I do remember sitting down, I can't remember how old I was – this is when it was first printed, 1929, and somebody helping me with it. But I know I had a lot of difficulty with it... (Gregory and Williams, 2000, p92)

This was an extraordinary book that used extra marks on vowels according to how they were pronounced (see Figure 4.2 below). Instructions at the beginning state that children will automatically transfer to normal print when ready, but that guessing was to be discouraged. Although unable to remember the precise rules behind reading each symbol, Gloria kept this book alongside all her other most treasured first texts.

It would be inappropriate to refer to the parents of this generation of readers as 'mediators' of English literacy, since they were often unable to speak English, let alone read or write it. Only Stanley, whose family spoke English as their first language, learned copperplate writing from his mother, which earned him the envy of his class-mates at school. However, everyone interviewed referred to their parents as role models of what they felt was truly literate behaviour in the widest sense. Thus, Minnie remembered her father as follows:

... but my father spoke about the world. He was fantastic... he read the Jewish Times, I think, and ... he used to read the Sunday paper right through and the very exclusive daily paper, he would read it. And there was a lady in the Burdett Road and she used to teach those foreign people to read and then he got naturalised after she taught him and he loved it and he learned to read all those papers. (Gregory and Williams, 2000, p83)

Figure 4.2: Phonoscript First Primer (1929)

The home literacy skills of these parents stood in stark contrast to their formal education in Britain. Aumie outlines in detail the knowledge of his parents which would have received no official recognition by school:

> The only education they would have had would have been Jewish religious education... my father in particular was considered quite a learned person in Jewish law, Jewish prayer and Jewish tradition. My mother was also fluent in reading Hebrew and Yiddish ... I remember constant disagreement when my father would reject some of the fairy-tales. 'Bubemeisers' we would call them – grandmother's tales. (Gregory and Williams, 2000, p83-4)

Gloria focused on the opportunities offered by her mother that she might become a member of the cultural, linguistic and literacy practices of a new country:

> My mother had ideas above her station. She liked to take me to Lyons Corner House and she taught me how to use a serviette... She would take me to matinées at the theatre and show me how to behave when you go out with other people... This was an education from my mother that few children of my age got, you know. (Gregory and Williams, 2000, p85)

In summary, this group of Londoners revealed worlds of literacy in their homes and communities that remained invisible to the schools they attended. In some respects, however, they were lucky. Although the Hebrew language and literacy played no part in official English school lessons, many of the children's teachers were themselves Jewish. They understood and shared the cultural and religious practices of the children they taught, respected them and, in some cases, facilitated continuation of these practices through school times and routines. At least one school in the area closed at lunch-time on Friday to allow children to celebrate the Sabbath with their families. More than half a century later, all this changed and Jewish practices were replaced by quite different invisible literacies in the community.

'Invisible' mediators of learning: Siblings and grandparents as skilled teachers of literacy

The second part of this chapter jumps to the end of the 20th and the first years of the 21st century and reveals the skill of two hitherto unrecognised groups of literacy 'teachers' outside school: siblings and grandparents. Although we have little reason to believe that teaching by these family members is a new phenomenon, both have hitherto been neglected in the parental involvement programmes, from the Bullock Report (1975) until the present day. Recently, however, a group of ethnographers in the UK and US have been working with teachers and families to reveal both the importance of the extended family in children's learning in multilingual contexts and ways in which these 'funds of knowledge' (Moll *et al*, 1992) can be used in the classroom (Gregory, Long and Volk, 2004). We describe some of this work and question the wisdom of a narrow interpretation of 'the family'. Instead of the official linear view of parents as 'experts' handing down their skills to children as 'novices', it presents both siblings and grandparents as 'teachers', and shows young children as active participators in community reading practices, sometimes novices, but sometimes skilled teachers themselves.

The families presented live in and around Spitalfields as did our earlier generation. However, they are no longer Jewish but of the Muslim faith and their origins lie in Bangladesh. Although Bangladeshi seamen had begun to arrive in London from the 1920s (Adams 1987), it was largely from the 1980s that the community began to establish itself, as had the Jewish families nearly one hundred years earlier. As in the Jewish community, supplementary education began with religion: a madrassah, where children were instructed in the tenets of Islam, and in the Arabic language, was started at the East London mosque in the Whitechapel High Street as early as the 1960s. By 1977, the East End Community School had also been set up to teach children literacy in Bengali (Asghar 1996). However, although by 1994 children of Bangladeshi British origin comprised between 80 to 100% of the intake of twenty-nine schools in the area (London Borough of Tower Hamlets 1994), these literacy practices remained by and large invisible to their teachers in the mainstream schools. The examples below unpick episodes which were typical of many taking place between both siblings and grandparents with young children at home.

Older siblings are imaginative yet strict teachers of literacy to young children. Numerous 'play school lessons' audiotaped by children aged between ten and eleven as they 'taught' their younger siblings at home reveal parallel but different literacies to those experienced in school as far as language, topic and even intonation are concerned. Older siblings all had very high expectations of behaviour which mirrored the children's community class and mosque lessons rather than school. Farjana (aged eleven) and Farhana (aged eight) typify a number of sibling dyads of a similar age as they learn together. The excerpt below follows those taking place in school on poetry which would have been familiar to both children:

> Farjana: OK very nice... Now we're going to do a short poem and memorise it. So it's not too hard... OK. Off you go... OK. Everybody should finish by now. Are you finished, Farhana?

Farhana: Yes.

Farjana: Let's see. It doesn't look finished. While you're doing yours, I'll read my poem, I done <?> OK. My poem.

I don't like working but I do like playing

Everytime I think of anything bad I start praying

I don't like working, but of course I like to <?> praying.

Now OK. I forgot to say something before all of you wrote your poems. If <?> every poem does not have to rhyme. It could be about anything, like I did about praying, playing and working. That's it. OK. I'll read my poem once again so we'll have an idea. But mine's do rhyme actually because I couldn't think of any other words. OK – my poem.... (repeats her poem). OK. Some of the words did rhyme, but in the real poems you don't quite... some poetry have it and some don't. So because when I didn't know all poems don't have to rhyme, I get the niggling thought ain't it strange why would it be called a poem if it does not rhyme. But I did find out all poems don't have to rhyme. OK Farhana have you finished yours?

Farhana: Yes.

Farjana: Would you like to read it to anybody?

Farhana: Traffic lights. The red light at the top says you have to stop
Red light and amber between say get ready for free
Green below says you can go.

Farjana: OK. Very good. But I'm sorry I didn't say that it doesn't have to rhyme and you had to think twice as much. Still it's very nice. OK. (Gregory 2005, p34-35)

Here we see a lesson taking place parallel to those the children would have witnessed in school. So only siblings or friends could participate, not parents or grandparents. Nor could parents have given such finely-tuned tutoring to enable Farhana to produce her own poem. The play-school lesson has both similarities and differences to the mainstream classroom. Although Farjana uses the content and language of her English school, her strict approach as well as the significance of prayer in her poem owe more to her Bengali or her Qur'anic class. Farhana is clearly the younger child, the novice, and is being taught by Farjana as expert. However, it is not that simple. Unlike the parent/ child relationship, we see how the older child herself learns by practising the task. We can, therefore, refer to this as a synergy whereby both children teach and learn from each other in a fluid yet structured way. It is clearly a different kind of teaching and learning from that which takes place between parent and child.

Grandparents, and particularly grandmothers, often play a crucial role in the lives of young Bangladeshi British children living in Britain (Jessel *et al*, 2004). Some grandparents in our study lived with their grandchildren and children, and others travelled the world, visiting grandchildren in the US, Canada and Australia. All saw their role as passing on important funds of linguistic, cultural and religious knowledge. Often they became yet more aware of their role owing to the loss of both language and traditions by the middle or parent generation, who often felt more comfortable in English. The illustrations in Figure 4.3 are taken from a longer video recording which shows six year-old Sumaya first gardening outside their house with her grandmother. During the gardening episode, we hear Sumaya's mother speaking to her in English in the background as Sumaya waters the trees and flowers. In the episode depicted below, however, a very different literacy practice is taking place with her grandmother. Sumaya is appropriately dressed, wearing the hijab, and her grandmother has spread out the rug upon which her book is placed. Speaking softly and melodically, Sumaya points to each phoneme, sounding it out in the classical Arabic she will meet when reading the Qur'an. She rarely makes a mistake, but when she does her grandmother corrects her firmly. Sumaya repeats the correction after her grandmother and continues immediately. She progresses from phonemes to digraphs and will gradually learn a large number of complex and varied blends of sounds before progressing to the Qur'an.

Although in many respects a contrast with the reading Sumaya will meet in school, she is learning a number of skills that she will be able to call upon: one-to-one correspondence, phonemic awareness, directionality (and its importance in different scripts), an eye for detail and an awareness of the importance of the written word, to name just a few. Sumaya's skill in learning both English and Qur'anic literacy successfully shows how two practices may complement rather than vie with each other as her competence grows in each.

Figure 4.3: Sumaya and her grandmother preparing for reading the Qur'an

The examples above begin to provide evidence that what counts as reading in children's lives outside school is *complex, cultural and personal* and that home and community practices vary widely in content, language and form. For children, such contrasting practices *can* be grafted successfully onto the official ways of the school. However, such 'grafting' or syncretism (Gregory, Long and Volk, 2004) of home and school practices is likely to be much more successful if teachers first *know* about children's home and community learning before building upon this in their classroom practice. Work on bilingual children's learning strategies in school and community settings (Kenner and Gregory, 2006-2007) indicates how children's experience of learning to read and write in Bengali can successfully underpin their English reading and vice versa, but for this to happen both mainstream and community class teachers need an awareness of each other's context. A closer exchange of curricula and methods of assessment between both would be a way forward for this knowledge to develop.

For teachers, the crucial question has always been: What enables some children to do this so successfully whilst others clearly struggle? In this chapter, I have argued that a vital key lies in the symbolic importance literacy has in an individual's life. Prinsloo and Stein (2005) refer to young children in South Africa as 'taking hold of reading' as they learn about the boundaries of reading and writing in classrooms. 'Taking hold' of literacy demands a confidence that extends well beyond any particular method or material of instruction. We now have evidence to show that, throughout the 20th and into the 21st centuries a great variety of literacy practices has provided children with a wealth upon which they may later draw. The examples in this chapter show ways in which children of all social and educational backgrounds have *taken hold* of literacy in ways that have usually remained invisible to their teachers in school.

Acknowledgement

My thanks are due to all the families participating in the Spitalfields Study and to the Economic and Social Research Council for funding on three projects (*Family Literacy History and Children's Reading Strategies at Home and at School, R000221186, 1994-6, Siblings as Mediators of Literacy in Two East London Communities, R000222487, 1998-9, Intergenerational Learning between Grandparents and Young Children in East London, R000220131, 2003-4 and Bilingual learning strategies in school and community contexts*) and the Leverhulme Foundation for a Research Fellowship 1997.

5

ENHANCING THE READING OF LOOKED AFTER CHILDREN AND YOUNG PEOPLE

Amanda Hatton and Jackie Marsh

The experiences of looked after children and young people are a pressing concern for those interested in issues of social exclusion and literacy. The phrase 'looked after' refers to children and young people in public care and includes those in foster homes and residential homes, in addition to those leaving the care system. National statistics in England point to the complex interaction of educational underachievement and negative effects on emotional, social and mental well-being which mean that looked after young people are more likely than their contemporaries to become unemployed, become teenage parents and end up in prison (SEU, 2005). In this chapter, we outline an innovative project in Derby City that aimed to enhance looked after children and young people's access to and engagement with books and other reading materials, the 'Read Away Derby' project. First, we outline the main issues relating to the reading practices and experiences of looked after children and the key features of the 'Read Away Derby project'. We move on to discuss the implications of the main findings of the evaluation of the project and to highlight the key factors that impacted on its success. We conclude by considering the work required to ensure that, in future, looked after children and young people can become confident and enthusiastic readers of a wide range of texts.

The educational attainment of looked after children and young people

The education of looked after children and young people is now a high priority in England. In March 2005, there were 60,900 looked after young children in England (DfES, 2005), many of whom are underachieving in national tests. In 2005, 10.8% of looked after young people achieved 5 GCSEs at A* to C, against a national figure of 56%. Attempts to improve the situation have been made over the last few decades.

The Children Act of 1989 established statutory powers and duties concerning the public care of children and young people and introduced National Standards. The Act required local authorities to look after children and young people who needed to be removed from their families, to place them in residential or foster care, and to act as their 'corporate parent'. 'Corporate parent' is defined as being 'the collective responsibility of local authorities to achieve good parenting' (DfEE/DoH, 1999:13). This parenting should address all aspects of children's lives, including health, safety, education and leisure. Concerns about the educational underachievement of looked after children and young people led to the Quality Protects Initiative (DoH, 1998), a programme of reforms to social services, launched in 1998 in order to address their educational needs. Targets were set for rates of young people leaving care in relation to GCSE qualifications, levels of school attendance and numbers of school exclusions. One of its objectives was 'to ensure that children looked after gain maximum life chance benefits from educational opportunities, health care and social care'(DoH, 1998.39). The Children Act of 2004, Section 52, introduced legislation that places a duty on local authorities to promote the educational achievement of looked after children and this came into effect in July, 2005.

The policy focus arose as a result of persisting concern about the educational underachievement of this group (Audit Commission, 1994; Social Services Inspectorate and Ofsted, 1995). A report from the Social Exclusion Unit on their educational under-attainment in England, *A Better Education for Children in Care: A Social Exclusion Unit Report*, identified the key factors contributing to this problem:

(i)   too many young people's lives are characterised by instability

(ii) young people in care spend too much time out of school or other places of learning

(iii) children in care do not have sufficient help with their education if they get behind

(iv) carers are not expected, nor equipped, to provide sufficient support and encouragement at home for learning and development and

(v) children in care need more help with their emotional, mental or physical health and wellbeing. (SEU, 2003:6)

Before moving into care, many of these young people have experienced traumatic events in their early lives, which impact upon their educational experiences and attainment. They may experience severe disruptions to schooling because of frequent moves and this can negatively affect their emotional, social and mental well-being (Jackson, 1988-9; SEU, 2003:). Francis (2000) observes that when a child goes into care, it can often be at a time when they are experiencing difficulties at school, so schooling can be one of the complex factors affecting their move into care. Looked after children are thirteen times more likely than others to be excluded from school (SEU, 2005). Low expectations and negative stereotypes have been found to be held of them in the educational system. Fletcher-Campbell and Hall (1990) found that looked after children and young people were stereotyped as low achievers and of low ability. Martin and Jackson (2002) point out that:

> It is generally assumed that children in residential or foster care are there because of personal deficit or character or behaviour, when most come into care as a result of family circumstances and through no fault of their own. (Martin and Jackson, 2002, p126).

Inevitably, these circumstances mean that educational underachievement becomes a systemic problem which affects other aspects of these children's lives. Goddard (2000, p80) observes that 'Research into outcomes for children who have left the care system has consistently shown that their educational disadvantage leads in turn to disadvantage in other areas of their lives'.

Literacy is a key area in the educational attainment of looked after children and young people. The government provides advice guidance for authorities about fulfilling their role as corporate parents in order to enable these young people to achieve educational success, suggesting that 'reading to them regularly improves their confidence with all their school work' (DfEE/DoH, 1999, p40). The National Minimum Standards for Children's Homes followed by noting the need for local authorities to ensure 'the provision of books, computers and library membership' in homes (DoH, 2002, p29). Statistics on looked after children and young people's attainment in national English tests offer a grim picture, as outlined in Table 1.

Table 1: Attainment of Looked After Children in Literacy/ English tests in England, 2005

	Looked-after-children	*All*
Key Stage 1: Number of children achieving Level 2 or above in:		
Reading	57%	85%
Writing	52%	82%
Key Stage 2: Number of children achieving Level 4 or above in English	42%	79%
Key Stage 3: Number of children achieving Level 5 or above in English	27%	74%

Table 1 indicates that the levels of looked after children and young people's attainment in literacy and English decrease as they get older, a pattern that has been noted in relation to wider educational achievement (Social Services Inspectorate and Ofsted, 1995).

Initiatives which have sought to tackle these issues have had varied success (SES, 2003). The most successful projects have been those that have enjoyed commitment from senior management within local authorities. In 2000 the Who Cares? Trust worked with the National Literacy Trust on the 'Right to Read' Project, which focused on providing residential centres with books and encouraging reading. The project was very successful and the involvement of libraries had a beneficial effect on children's reading practices. The critical factors in the success of this project were found to be the commitment of senior management in the local authority and the enthusiasm of the project staff (WCT, 2001).

A recent Ofsted report (Ofsted, 2006) indicates that local authority provision for looked after children and young people is improving. The report comments that in 2005:

> Councils performed well in the field of education and three quarters of councils deliver services that are well above or consistently above minimum requirements. In the best examples, there is a strong and positive partnership with schools and support services which is built on shared and aspirational targets for improvement. (Ofsted, 2006, p8)

These features can be seen in the case study of one project focused on promoting reading amongst looked after children and young people in Derby City.

Read Away Derby

Over some years, Derby City has adopted a range of strategies to enhance the educational attainment of looked after children. The city's Gatsby Project began in 2000. It aims to improve the educational attainment and life chances of children and young people in public care (and also those who have left care) and to develop sustainable strategies to ensure that these improvements can be maintained beyond the end of the project in 2006. The Gatsby Project promotes multi-professional working and since 2000 Derby's Library, Education and Social Services have focused on promoting access to books and reading for these young people. The Read Away Derby project linked into this well-established framework. The project ran from 2003 to January 2006 and aimed to:

- improve the long-term access to books and reading for all looked after children and young people in Derby

- develop a book and reading culture for all looked after children and young people in Derby – that can a) be sustained after the funding has ended and b) be a model of good multi-agency practice

- complement and support through books and reading Derby's drive to improve the educational outcomes for children and young people in care.

The Read Away Derby project was delivered by Read On, Write Away! (ROWA! – see http//www.rowa.org.uk). ROWA! is a literacy initiative set up as an Independent Partnership, working to develop community-focused literacy and basic skills initiatives in Derby City and Derbyshire. It has an international reputation for its wide range of innovative and exciting projects. Over the last eight years, ROWA! has developed community and school-based literacy projects that span 'cradle to grave'. Targeting areas of high social need, ROWA! works in collaboration with a range of partners, including regional and national organisations such as The National Literacy Trust. Read Away Derby is the second project run by ROWA! that has focused on the reading practices of looked after children and young people. The first, the Utterly Sensational Books and Reading Project for You, Me, Us! (US! Project) was set up by ROWA! in September 2001, initially by Terry Smith (see Marsh, 2004) and pioneered many of the approaches later adopted by the Read Away Derby Project. These approaches, categorised under different project strands, are summarised in Table 2.

Table 2: Strategies used by Read Away Derby to enhance access to reading materials and promote enjoyment in reading for looked after children and young people

Strand	Objectives	Activities
Work with foster carers and children in foster care	■ To help children and young people in foster care to develop their interest in literacy. ■ To encourage foster carers to interest and involve children and young people in the library. ■ To facilitate access to and ownership of books for children and young people in care. ■ To develop family placement workers' understanding of issues related to literacy and looked after children.	■ Book parties were held at Derby branch libraries, to which were invited all young people in foster care and their carers, and all young people in residential care. A poet attended the party, carers received advice about reading and books, library promotion, and time with librarians. Each young person received a book they chose for themselves. ■ In the second phase of the project, book tokens were sent to all young people in foster care, in a gift pack with bookmarks, information about libraries and recommended books. ■ Information about books and reading was sent to fostering social workers. ■ At a pantomime event run in partnership with the Foster Care Association, books were given to young people in care and their siblings. ■ The ROWA! Bus offered interactive computer activities for young people and their carers. ■ At the Young Achievers Award, book tokens were given to young people in care and care leavers.

Table 2: Strategies used by Read Away Derby to enhance access to reading materials and promote enjoyment in reading for looked after children and young people (continued)

Strand	Objectives	Activities
Work with young parents to be, sexually active and pre-sexually active young people	■ To develop specific book boxes which provided factual and fictional books about pregnancy, childbirth, parenting and linked options, in order to raise awareness of young parents and young people in care who are sexually active or considering sexual activity. ■ To develop workers' understanding of how these resources can be used with young parents and young people in care who are sexually active or considering sexual activity. ■ To ensure that young parents (looked after or care leavers) receive information about using the library. ■ To develop young parents' awareness of family literacy practices. ■ To encourage young parents to consider returning to accredited learning.	■ Residential Child Care Workers used the books with young people on a one to one basis. ■ A collection of books was also given to the fostering team. ■ A more extensive collection was given to the LAC nurses to use across the homes and with young people in foster care. ■ The LAC nurse spent time with the Leaving Care Service, social workers, the fostering and adoption team and the Residential Educational Forum meeting, to talk through the use of the Facts and Feelings books ■ A Facts and Feelings collection was also given to the Leaving Care Service for workers to give to young parents. ■ To encourage young parents in care or who have recently left care with their reading, and to share books with their children, book collections were put in the Leaving Care Service centre. There is now an active book-borrowing system in the centre, set up and managed by one of the workers, and refreshed and funded by the centre. Encouragement is given to boys and young men to participate. ■ Basic Skills Agency 'Speaking and listening guides' were put into backpacks for young parents.

Table 2: Strategies used by Read Away Derby to enhance access to reading materials and promote enjoyment in reading for looked after children and young people (continued)

Strand	Objectives	Activities
Training/ workshops	■ To develop understanding of a range of practitioners who work with looked after children and young people with regard to the importance of literacy.	■ Multi-agency workshops were offered for foster carers and Residential Child Care Workers: sessions dealt with ways to encourage reading, education issues, exclusion, placement and information about using the library.
	■ To provide practitioners with strategies to promote literacy with looked after children and young people.	■ Sessions were held for respite foster carers in conjunction with the Toy library.
	■ To work towards mainstreaming activities by involving statutory services e.g. library.	■ ICT courses were provided for foster carers – and for a Residential Child Care Worker on extra time who would then cascade to workers in other homes
	■ To ensure that looked after children and young people have a voice in issues regarding the training of practitioners.	■ ICT sessions were provided in two children's homes
		■ The project co-ordinator and the senior children's librarian attended children's homes team meetings and Residential Education Forum meetings to disseminate information about project activity and consult with partners about best ways of delivery
		■ There was input into Advisory Service training for foster carers and social workers: a project consultant provided a session on books and enjoying reading.

Table 2: Strategies used by Read Away Derby to enhance access to reading materials and promote enjoyment in reading for looked after children and young people (continued)

Strand	Objectives	Activities
Focused work with children's homes	■ To help young people in residential care to develop their interest in literacy. ■ To facilitate access to and ownership of books for children and young people in residential care. ■ To encourage residential workers to interest and involve children and young people in residential care in literacy activities and the use of the library. ■ To ensure that each children's home receives input which meets their specific needs, based on baseline assessment of these needs. ■ To provide inspirational events which promote engagement in literacy. ■ To ensure that looked after children and young people have a voice in the activities planned to promote literacy.	■ Book collections worth about £100 each were placed in each home. ■ Book parties with a poet were organised in the libraries; and an event at a pantomime was organised in collaboration with the Foster Carers Association. ■ Book tokens were given to foster carers to use as they chose. ■ Opportunities were provided for young people to choose their own book on a visit to a supplier, or to have book tokens – young people also helped choose the collections for the homes. ■ In visits to the homes by the project co-ordinator, children were able to choose books to keep. ■ Bookplates and ROWA! bookmarks were given along with the gift books. ■ A buddy book buying scheme was introduced – book tokens were given to young people to choose a book for themselves and one for their key worker. ■ Book tokens were awarded as prizes at the Young Achievers Awards. ■ RAD project staff and librarians visited homes and talked informally with young people about their reading, providing opportunities to choose books. ■ The Big Flick: a selection of magazines were sent to each home. ■ Potty Poet sessions (poet visits) were held in homes.

As Table 2 shows, the project included work with both foster carers and children's homes. This chapter focuses on the work with children's homes.

The Read Away Derby Project was externally evaluated using several methods, including documentary analysis of various reports and project resources, statistical analysis of take-up figures, observations of Read Away Derby sessions in residential homes and semi-structured, face-to-face and telephone interviews with professionals involved in the education and care of looked after children. In addition, face-to-face, semi-structured interviews were conducted with fourteen looked after children and young people. Amanda Hatton (2005) interviewed eleven residents in children's homes during the life of the Read Away Derby project aged from ten to seventeen, to identify their reading practices and interests. The interviews in both studies were taped and transcribed. This chapter draws from the two sets of data to explore the ways in which approaches which were successful enhanced the literacy lives of the young participants.

Access and use of texts in residential homes

Martin and Jackson (2002) researched the experiences of a group of high achievers who had experienced public care. Over half of those interviewed commented on the dearth of practical resources in residential homes and the authors reported that: 'Many homes lacked basic necessities such as books, a desk or a quiet room in which to do home-work or study' (Martin and Jackson, 2002, p126). The Who Cares? Trust 'Book of My Own' project further demonstrated how few children in residential care have access to books or have any of their own. Having few books can diminish interest in reading. As Rees states:

> Books and other publications are an important part of the environment. The availability or absence of a good choice of books and reading material gives a strong message about education. (Rees, 2001, p276)

Accordingly, a major strategy of the Read Away Derby project was to enhance the resources of children's homes to foster reading. Selections of books, comics and magazines were provided by the project and by Derby Library Services. In some cases, residents were involved in selecting the books themselves. Project and library staff also engaged in dialogue with Residential Child Care Workers to ensure that the resources provided were appropriately displayed and used.

In some homes, strong reading cultures already prevailed, developed over years by committed senior managers. During the project, this good practice permeated many other homes, as seen on visits made towards the end of the projects, where vibrant reading cultures were in evidence. Bookshelves displayed a range of appealing books. Staff talked about how they rotated reading material and engaged the children in conversations about their reading and this stimulated reading. Members of staff noted the increased appetite for reading:

> I've had good feedback because some of the books that they've brought, they've really took to them and they've actually engaged in reading them... they're more interested that they were before, anyway.

> We had bookcases before, but they were very much outdated... They're interested now because they're more graphic and more 'comicy' looking.

> They're actually taking some of the books away and we're finding them in their rooms, that's says something, doesn't it, if you find them in their rooms?

Key to the success of the project was the role of training for Residential Child Care Workers; the provision of enhanced resources alone would not have been sufficient. Intensive sessions of up to an hour were in some cases enough to enhance the workers' knowledge of children's literature:

> Staff in here would definitely benefit from [training] because I came away even from that hour session with a different focus. The kind of books that were on offer, I didn't even know about the books that were on offer, these high interest books.

The choice of texts also contributed to the project's success. Project workers had involved the young people in the selection of books, but they also had a good knowledge of children's literature so could identify relevant, engaging texts, many relating to popular cultural interests. The project had included comics, magazines and electronic texts in the resources offered. Marsh and Millard (2000) note a 'tendency amongst educationalists to privilege interactions with story books above other types of literacy practices' (Marsh and Millard, 2000:69). This model was challenged in this project, with other texts, such as comics and magazines, being equally valued. This was important because the cared for young people expressed a preference for a wide variety of reading material, including online texts of films and computer games (Hatton, 2005).

Hatton (2005) identified two of the most popular titles enjoyed by the looked after children and young people she interviewed as the 'Harry Potter' and 'Tracey Beaker' series. It is of note that these narratives are also found in popular cultural forms such as films, TV series, magazines, stickers and other merchandise and that both narratives feature a boy or girl hero with no parents, living in an institutionalised setting. Both these factors may be significant in these choices. However, the reading patterns and practices noted by Hatton (2005) were also prevalent in a study of the reading choices of a wider population (Hall and Coles, 1999) and we would not wish to suggest that the textual preferences of looked after children and young children are very different from those of other demographic groups. Nevertheless, the book and the television version of the 'Tracey Beaker' stories were rated as significant by the young people and by the Residential Child Care Workers. One worker commented that when the television programme was on, the children 'sit absolutely glued to it until it's finished'. Looked after children and young people need to be able to access texts that reflect their life experiences and enable them to enjoy the 'life-to-text' and 'text-to-life' experiences (Cochran-Smith, 1984) that so enhance narrative satisfaction.

In the Read Away Derby (RAD) project, Residential Child Care Workers were encouraged to read to children. Hatton's (2005) analysis of looked after children and young people's experiences of reading shows that they found being read to a memorable experience. The majority of those interviewed could recall parents, a teacher, a past carer and workers reading to them. One of the young men interviewed, for example, who had reading difficulties, remembered the staff in a children's home reading *Harry Potter* to him. Hatton also noted that during her visits to homes that housed older children, the staff did not read them fiction but newspapers and then discussed articles with them. Such exposure is vital in fostering an interest in a wide range of texts.

Reading for information as well as pleasure was another strand of the project. RAD ensured that each home had a 'Facts and Feelings' collection, a set of books about emotional, health and social issues, such as sexuality and pregnancy. This collection was also placed with the Leaving Care Service and with the Looked After Children's (LAC) Nurse, who used the books in a targeted manner with pregnant girls and young people who were sexually active. The LAC Nurse found the books about pregnancy useful when working with teenage mothers, some of whom had used the books to find out about what was happening at each stage of their pregnancy. These texts had helped the girls to feel less isolated. A care leaver reported:

> *I borrowed loads, they were brilliant. Oh, there were those ones about being pregnant and it was like reading my own life back, it was so good. When you're going through things as a teenage mum... you think that you must be*

the only one feeling stressed and depressed and feeling the things that you feel, but reading that book, it was actually a true story about a girl's actual experience and it was just everything that I felt about hospital and the way people look at you when you're a teenage mum and how at first you might feel a bit trapped until you get used to it...I couldn't put it down.

These pleasurable and informative textual experiences are vital to developing long-term reading habits.

Use of library services

Research by Jackson and Martin (1998) which focused on the experiences of young people who have been in care and succeeded in education found that those who had progressed well were the keen readers and members of a library. A strong emphasis of the work in Derby was the development of partnerships between the children's homes and community libraries. Visits by librarians to the homes provided opportunities for dialogue and developing relationships. The librarians provided incentives to visit the library, such as vouchers for free CD and DVD loans. Staff in many of the homes reported that they visited the library with children and young people more regularly as a result. In some homes, it became a regular event; in others it was organised as requested by the children themselves.

Library fines occasionally deterred young people from going to the library. Accumulating large fines appeared to be a regular occurrence. In the words of one young person who was a care leaver: 'I lived in children's homes and when you move from one children's home to the other, things get stolen and lost and stuff'. However, swift intervention by library staff meant that fines were waived and library visits re-established.

A particularly innovative resource used by Derby Library Services was the 'Reading Rocket' bus, which parked regularly outside one of the residential homes for younger children. The bus was attractively decorated, the interior designed especially for use with children, furnished with compact book-shelves and seating. The children who visited it said they preferred the bus to the library, as it was less intimidating. Residential staff reported that those who did not access mainstream education felt self-conscious when they visited a large public building like the library. Given the importance for looked after children to feel secure in places and spaces, initiatives such as the 'Reading Rocket' are worth emulating.

A Book of My Own

One of the most successful strands of the project was giving books to looked after young people to keep. Many had owned very few of their own books. As Rees (2001:277) found: 'Few children in residential care routinely have access to books... in contrast to children at home, many of whom have dozens before they even go to school.'

Hatton found in her 2005 study that when children and young people did have books of their own, they often became strongly emotionally attached to them, as they resonated with their past lives with their families. One of the girls, aged fifteen, commented about the single book she possessed, 'I don't know why, but I just look at the pictures.' She added, '...it was just something my mum had and I liked the picture on the front of it so I got it.' Similarly a girl of twelve said she owned about ten books and that they were, 'Just, like, the ones from when I was a baby, when I was little'. Another boy, aged thirteen, reported that he had about twenty books and that, 'I have had some of them since I was nearly two.' As Bald (1982) has pointed out, 'A child's own collection of books can provide an important source of stability, satisfaction and personal involvement' (Bald, 1982:20). So the project offered young people an opportunity to build up their own collection of treasured texts. They said they had read and re-read the books they were given and that they enjoyed receiving a book of their own because, as one young girl put it, 'You can read it again and again and again'.

There was evidence that the reading material had contributed to children's emotional well-being. Some of those interviewed mentioned the effects of reading on stress: *'It calms you down'*, and the benefits of reading about events and issues that related to their own situations. The Tracey Beaker novels by Jacqueline Wilson were particular favourites. One young boy found that reading books helped him come to terms with his mother's death. This important aspect of reading is often overlooked and its significance is even more powerful in relation to the emotional needs of looked after children. As Coles (1999) observes:

> The literacy debate must be expanded to include specific questions on what children need to think and feel about, what they emotionally need to acquire or reject as they learn to read and write. (Coles, 1999, np)

Many of those who took part in the project greatly enjoyed choosing a book of their own. Visits to bookshops were especially welcomed. These findings correlate with previous studies. For example, interviews were conducted with looked after young people as part of the evaluation of the Taking Care of

Education Project, co-ordinated by the National Children's Bureau and funded by the Gatsby Charitable Foundation (Harker *et al*, 2003) and they were asked about their experiences of education. Their perceptions focused on the instability experienced through being in care, which included unsettling placement changes and mid-term school transfers. They said they felt they would benefit from the 'provision of quiet study space and access to computers, key books and educational resources' in homes. Opportunities for children to purchase their own books was seen as a relevant factor in encouraging educational progress' (Harker *et al*, 2003, p96). So as well as having access to texts in homes and being given books of their own, it is important for looked after children and young people to be encouraged to visit bookshops, where they can enjoy browsing and buying books for themselves.

Multi-stranded, longitudinal projects

Following the model of the US! Project, the Read Away Derby project had several related strands: book collections to homes, books given to children to keep, one-off events such as author and poet visits and book collections given to the Leaving Care Service. Rather than dissipating the energy of a project, it appeared that the synergy developed through these parallel strands enhanced the experiences of the young people. The longitudinal nature of the project meant that if they remained in the care system for some time, they could enjoy a variety of encounters with texts. Hatton reflects on the experiences of one young woman:

> Sharon was involved in the project in a variety of ways and was able to use a selection of books, both fiction and non-fiction. I first met this young woman in one of the residential children's homes during one of my visits to talk about books and reading. I spent time with her and was able to involve her in discussions about what would be appropriate choices of books to bring into the children's homes.
>
> In discussing her attitudes to reading, Sharon showed she was a versatile consumer of a variety of reading materials. She enjoyed reading, particularly poetry and her favourite book at that time was Tracey Beaker. She had also enjoyed reading adult fiction, particularly Lovely Bones. As part of the discussion she recommended a selection of favourite magazines. This was very useful and informed project activity as I was able to send out an appropriate selection of magazines to the children's homes following her recommendations.
>
> During our discussion Sharon made recommendations about what sort of books young people might like to have on the bookshelves in the children's

homes. These included: the Tracey Beaker books; other Jacqueline Wilson books; the Harry Potter books; thrillers; poetry books and short stories. When I made the selection of books for the children's home I was able to include these books, along with other recommendations from other young people. I also used this as a guideline for providing books to other children's homes and the Leaving Care Service.

I next met Sharon at the Leaving Care Service when I delivered their selection of books and as she was there, she opened the box to see what I had brought. Her immediate reaction was one of enthusiasm and she was pleased to see some of the books she had suggested. Her response was: 'Hey, these are all the ones that I chose. I told you to get these'.

Sharon later became pregnant and had input from the Looked After Children's nurse, who was able to use some of the Facts and Feelings books with her. The fiction books in particular were the 'Megan' series and the practical books were also useful. Sharon particularly used 'The Rough Guide to Teenage Pregnancy', which she used on a daily basis as a reference book to follow the stages of her pregnancy and look up the terms used in her ante-natal appointments. After the birth of her baby she was given a backpack, which included books for the baby, a fiction book for the mum, a baby's first year calendar and a practical book on parenting in the early months.

The combination of being multi-stranded and longitudinal appears to enhance the quality of projects that promote the enjoyment of reading for looked after children and young people, although other factors contributed to the project's overall success (for a full evaluation of the project, see Marsh, Hatton and Kings, 2006). Some of these factors are identified in the last section of this chapter and the implications for research, policy and practice are considered.

Success factors and future directions

A number of factors ensured the success of the Read Away Derby project:

(a) *Effective partnership working*

The regular meetings of the Read Away Derby Project Group enabled an effective partnership of key organisations to be built up from the start. The project was able to build successfully on the strong corporate partnership already established in Derby City through the Gatsby Project. This enabled the identification of a corporate vision for the promotion of reading for looked after children and young people in Derby. There are shared priorities and clear agreement about the way forward. This is an important factor in the work of effective authorities (Ofsted, 2006).

(b) *Clear aims and objectives that were reviewed appropriately*
The project began with a clear set of aims and objectives. These were reviewed regularly and adapted where necessary. Such flexibility of aims and objectives is necessary when working with groups with complex and changing needs and the Read Away Derby Project Group responded well to external challenges and possibilities.

(c) *Sustainability of the project built into its conception.*
The future sustainability of the project was considered by the Read Away Derby Project Group from the start. This means that certain plans were made early on to ensure that strategies were put in place to extend beyond the life of the project, such as linking each children's home with a neighbourhood library and a named library contact and depositing collections of up to 25 library books in each home, to be exchanged every six to eight weeks.

(d) *Project design*
The design of the project was flexible enough to allow bespoke sessions which met the needs of particular homes. Given the varied needs of the residential homes in Derby City, this was a useful approach.

(e) *Subject knowledge of the Project Co-ordinator*
The project was successful because the Project Co-ordinator and the Project Consultants brought into the project at various points had sound knowledge of children's literature and were aware of the need for the collections to include books which reflected the children's own cultural interests.

(f) *Use of a variety of materials*
The project did not just focus on books but recognised that children have a wide range of reading interests, including comics, magazines and textual practices embedded in new technologies. All are highly motivating (Marsh and Millard, 2005).

(g) *Use of creative approaches*
The project developed a range of creative approaches to its work. In particular, one-off events to stimulate interest in books and reading were very effective, such as the 'Potty Poet' visits to children's homes.

The Read Away Derby project, along with the US! Project before it, have important lessons for researchers, policy makers and professionals concerned with the reading practices of looked after children and young people. First, more extensive research is needed into their reading practices so that assumptions are not made about the nature of texts with which young people want to engage. Without this knowledge, professionals cannot draw effectively on children's 'funds of knowledge' (Moll *et al*, 1992).

Second, national policy needs to take account of the need to fund multi-stranded, longitudinal projects that can effectively involve a range of partners. Indeed, in the long-term, project funding is insufficient; what is needed is substantive funding for each of the partner organisations to mainstream these activities on a permanent basis. For example, the funding to establish named and trained children's librarians who would be designated to specific residential homes would normally be unavailable to local authorities in the present economic climate. Yet such funding could significantly encourage looked after children to use the libraries. More long-term funding should also be available to provide a range of good fiction and non-fiction, comics and magazines and electronic texts in residential homes, with the children actively involved in selecting the resources. Another significant contributor to the project's success was providing books for the individual children to keep and although residential homes can allocate a proportion of their budget for this purpose, discrete central funding is needed for this to happen in all cases. Finally, this project demonstrated the value of providing regular training for Residential Child Care Workers and foster carers on the promotion of reading enjoyment. Training could be usefully extended to Children's Social Care Workers. All these strategies need a financial as well as policy commitment from the Government if the aims of The Children Act 2004 are to be fully achieved.

Conclusion

This chapter has outlined some of the successful features of the Read Away Derby project. It has also explored wider issues that are pertinent to the reading practices and attitudes of looked after children and young people. There have been many improvements in local authority provision for this group in recent years (Ofsted, 2006), but there is scope for improving literacy to raise attainment, achievement and aspirations. Professionals working in organisations involved in the social care and education of looked after children and young people can strive to apply some of the knowledge acquired from previous analyses of practice (SEU, 2003), but future work can only succeed if it receives sufficient Government funding. If the economic implications of national policy are not fully taken into account by the policy-makers, then these young people may continue to underachieve and miss the opportunities to engage in a wide and rich range of reading practices.

Note

Read Away Derby was funded by the Paul Hamlyn Foundation, the Gatsby Foundation and the Teenage Pregnancy Strategy in Derby, with match-funded worker time from Derby Library, Education and Social Services. Amanda Hatton was the Project Co-ordinator for the Read Away Derby project and Jackie Marsh was the external evaluator.

Acknowledgements

We would like to thank the partner organisations of the Read Away Project Group, including Read On, Write Away! and the Gatsby Project, for agreeing to share the findings of the 'Read Away Derby' project in this chapter. We are very grateful to all the looked after children and young people and Residential Child Care Workers who agreed to talk to us about their experiences during the project and whose voices are heard in this chapter. Finally, we would like to thank the Paul Hamlyn Foundation for funding the project.

6

'I SORT OF READ TO BE MIDDLE CLASS AND THEN I SORT OF READ TO BE GAY': THE READING PRACTICES AND IDENTITIES OF GAY MEN

Mark Vicars

Literacy... becomes pleasurable when it exceeds social utility, leaves behind the familiar and the well rehearsed, and moves into uncharted territories where loss, discomfort, playfulness – even sexuality – can be fully expressed. (Silin, 2003, p.261)

Introduction

This chapter considers the ways in which texts were used by a gay man during his adolescence to perform identity work. Studies into the experiences of lesbian, gay and bisexual youth suggest that literacy behaviour, involving literary fictions, can be helpful in repositioning their knowledge of self away from the social margins (Blackburn, 2002; 2003).

The story of reading that I want to share is taken from a study that sought to address the significant knowledge gap about the reading practices of a culturally marginalised community. Five gay men took part in group interviews over seven months in order to explore the role played by texts in the construction of queer identities. The prologue to this study is drawn from my own experiences and I have taken excerpts from Mother's (a pseudonym) story that try to represent our travels beyond the surface of a range of texts. At various stages in the interviews, Mother described himself as a 37-year-old, white, middle-class, camp, out, gay/queer man. I understand each of these identifications as being culturally produced and throughout this chapter adopt the stance that 'biographies of ordinary people can be considered as constructions (or fabrications) in which the imagination plays an important role' (Appadurai, 1996, p54).

Fone (1983) has suggested how gay men could employ their imaginations in reading and interpreting texts to overcome the difficulties of living in a culture that makes being gay a problem. He posits the idea that a queerly positioned, differently nuanced reading of text can:

1)   ... suggest a place where it is safe to be gay: where gay men can be free from the outlaw status society confers upon us, where homosexuality can be revealed and spoken of without reprisal, and where homosexual love can be consummated without concern for the punishment or scorn of the world;

2)   ... imply the presence of gay love and sensibility in a text that otherwise makes no explicit statement about homosexuality. (Fone, 1983, p13)

These ideas indicate how a positional and perspectival reading of texts 'can expose the assumptions of universal heterosexuality' (Kennard, 1986, p77). They usefully problematise the relationship between text and reader and re-focus attention on how texts sometimes get read in ways other than the author intended.

Prologue

In the summer of 1978, Grease was the word and Sylvester, a gay drag performer, was belting out his signature disco anthem *You Make Me Feel* (*Mighty Real*), remaking and bringing the presence of black and gay culture visible to mainstream audiences. In the same summer I, along with countless others, queued at local cinemas to watch repeatedly as John Travolta and cast represented heterosexuality at its most seductive and compelling. I bought into the mythic and the ritualised, but as I fell into longing for that fictional lifeworld, the intensity of my desire whilst momentarily (Mighty Real), also made me feel strangely left out and left over. With each viewing I found myself reading the movie in my own way. My interpretative stance was inserting the possibility of there being a gay presence in a movie that to all intents and purposes was all about the pleasures of being heterosexual.

Althusser (1968) has spoken about the possibilities and pleasures afforded by reading against the normative messages encoded in texts and my wayward imagination was performing what he has called a 'symptomatic reading'. A 'symptomatic reading' is:

> ...an interpretive strategy that searches not only for the structural dominants in a text but most importantly, for absences and omissions that are an indication of what the dominant ideology seeks to repress, contain or marginalise. (Kotsopoulous, 2006)

Increasingly affected by my attraction to the same sex, I playfully reconstructed the movie's narrative in my mind to include what I was feeling, thinking and wanting to happen. In the 110 minutes it took to watch *Grease* I had not only faced the secret that I had been partially keeping from myself and completely concealing from others, but found myself using my furtive desire to supplement (Derrida, 1976) the boy meets girl narrative with what I can only describe now as a gay interpretation. Leaving the cinema at the end of the movie in the company of my sister and her friends, the conversations were all about the romance between the main characters Danny and Sandy. I knew better than to agree with them about how gorgeous Danny was and instead found myself talking about the car. By the end of the summer of 1978, I had seen the film eight times and had fallen madly in love with the character of Danny Zuko. *Grease* had generated a yearning for something I felt was missing yet, hooked, I went back for more masochistic dissatisfaction – and I was not alone.

> Mother: *I remember going to see Grease in my early teens and the next day at school felt incredibly emotional and really sad about the whole thing. I just felt that everything was lacking, I felt alone in a story... that is what it was like being a queer kid. The aftershocks of that movie lived with me for quite some time, I was wanting something... I remember sitting in the bath sobbing my eyes out. I wasn't part of that world, I wasn't part of any world. All I wanted to do was to make myself small, very, very small so I could slip by unnoticed.*

Sylvester, on the other hand, didn't require the same kind of labour. A hybrid performance of male/female, gender ambiguous, sexually indeterminate and to my naïve gaze the embodiment of Other (Fine, 1994), he was a marked contrast to the normative expressions of desire represented within the flickering frames of that globally triumphant movie. Sylvester was a carnivalesque event (Bakhtin, 1984) in my suburban world. His parody of gender roles and mocking of the authority of 'the prohibitions of usual life' (Bakhtin 1984, p. 15) helped me to understand that there was another way of being and seeing the world. However, at the age of eleven he exceeded my capacity for interpretation, but as a troubling signifier of sexual difference he surpassed my naïve expectations of what a possible life might be and in a way that the coupling of Danny and Sandy never did.

Novel gazing – reading as a way of coming to know about the self

During the next few years I developed an interpretive strategy in my reading of texts that successfully displaced what has been called the heterosexual imaginary (Ingraham, 1997), those heterosexual forms of meaning that make it almost impossible to consider being anything but straight. Adolescent gay sexual identification is often a hidden process (Vicars, 2005) that can mean that homosexuality dare not normally announce its presence within the context of the everyday life of school. Quinlivan and Town (1999) have commented how 'School communities seldom have to move beyond the personal deficit model in attempting to meet the needs of lesbian and gay youth' (p251), and throughout adolescence the stigma attached to being gay meant books and movies became the main instruments of my confession. I increasingly began to read for recognition. I wanted to know if there was any way out of what I thought at the time was my particular problem and what had to be a mistake. Appleyard (1990) has suggested that young adult readers read fiction to identify with the characters and to think about their own lives in relation to those presented in the text. If, as Sumara (1996) claims, 'during and following acts of engagement with literary fictions various identity transformations occur' (Sumara, 1996,p.85), then it is possible to imagine how a different form of textual occupancy can re-make the disciplined spaces of everyday life as 'smooth' and 'habitable' (de Certeau, 1984) for gay youth. Texts offer a possibility for getting lost in other worlds but for lesbian, gay or bisexual readers they can also provide transport to a new way of understanding about themselves in relation to their sexuality. Texts can become a means through which to travel beyond the everyday all-encompassing world of heterosexuality. Texts in the hands and minds of lesbian, gay and bisexual youth can become a powerful tool for exploring their sexuality in a safe manner and for discovering about being lesbian, gay or bisexual without the fear of reprisal.

> Mother: *Texts leave an indelible print and there were some days I would leap back into the book of the moment and pray to be left alone, It was a way to survive. Having the life I wanted, needed, was reading about it, and I read myself into that place. Textual worlds were a band-aid that helped me hold it together. I was afraid of rejection, of not being accepted, of not understanding, of not having any role models who actually said to me gay was good.*

The isolation experienced by Mother is common to many youths who find themselves questioning their sexuality but who are in situations where they cannot show who they really are or talk about what they are experiencing.

Despite the changing attitudes surrounding the discourse on homosexuality in society at large, and the moves to combat homophobia in education (DfES, 2000, 2004), there is still 'little or no opportunity for the homosexually orientated adolescent to discover what it means to be homosexual' (Martin and Heterick, 1988, p167) in schools. All there is are schoolyard jokes and pejorative remarks.

> Mother: *Believe me, picking up on being a poof very early on in life isn't good thing. I knew I was being marked as different very early on, or as the kids on the estate where I lived put it 'a fat poof'.*

Rofes (1995) has talked about the heresy of growing up as a sissy boy. As a favourite fictional character of mine, the Cowardly Lion from *Wizard of Oz* (Metro-Goldwyn-Mayer, 1939), declared, 'It's sad, believe me missy, when you're born to be a sissy, without the vim or verve'. 'Queer', 'poofter', 'lezzie', 'dyke 'and 'that's so gay' are just a few of the insults hurled at students who experience the consequences of not being 'straight' or not being 'straight' enough. Pejorative utterances are powerful tools in the heteronormative arsenal and can speak volumes about how the pervasive ideology of heteronormativity is encountered within school life (Herr, 1997). Warner (1993) coined the term 'heteronormativity' to describe how heterosexuality is institutionalised and legitimated by being believed to be the only 'normal' and valid sexual orientation. Heterosexuality becomes universal and 'natural' whereas other forms of sexuality get thought of as unnatural, odd, perverse and queer.

Studies investigating the experience of sexual minorities in schools (Rivers, 2000, 2001; Ellis and High, 2004) paint a dismal picture of what is happening to young people in schools who identify or who are identified as being lesbian, gay or bisexual. The presumption of heterosexuality often regulates what can and cannot be said and can effectively silence students who are questioning their sexuality. Mac an Ghaill (1994) found in his study *Masculinities, Sexualities and Schooling* that the gay youth he spoke to 'emphasised the personal isolation, confusion, marginalisation and alienation' and that if they had no positive references 'they tended to internalise ambivalent negative messages about themselves as gay men' (Mac an Ghaill, 1994, p161). Perhaps then, it is not so peculiar to imagine how texts for lesbian, gay or bisexual students offer a place where they can spontaneously express themselves and find answers to questions such as 'Where do I belong?' and 'How do I fit in?', questions that echo Mother's motivation and purpose for reading.

Mother: *...I think quite early on I was going out of my way to seek certain texts. I started to seek out texts that I thought would be important to my future life. I was looking for things in texts in order to become a gay man 'cos nobody was there to teach me. I remember reading from the canon of queer literature: Forster's* Maurice, *Baldwin's* Giovanni's Room *and Auden's* The Temple. *I was hoping for some epiphany about being gay. I am now able to look back and understand how those texts were important, very important. There was so much I was unable to articulate at that time. Texts helped me to start being comfortable within myself.*

So is it possible to imagine a reading encounter in which there is more than mere words and letters generating meaning? The notion invites reflection on the wider social and cultural contexts that frame the reading of texts. This chapter focuses next on what Mother had to say about how, as a gay adolescent reader, he inscribed texts with his own experiences, attitudes and purposes in order to create his own meanings (Philo and Miller, 2000).

Between a rock and a hard place

Mother: *I didn't have a strong identity as a working class lad and my feelings of marginality came from my class, my gender and my sexuality. All my brother's friends played football, were hard as nails and used to beat the shit out of everybody. I was desperate to be middle-class. I honed in on middle-class kids and read literature 'cos that is what it was to be posh. I sort of read to be middle-class and then I sort of read to be gay.*

In interviews, Mother spoke about growing up as a working-class kid in small town middle England in the 1980s and how he felt increasingly split between the life he was living and the one he wanted to live. Knowing that he would never fully reify the model of emphatic masculinity that was being ritually performed through what Mac an Ghaill (1994) has called 'The three Fs – fighting, fucking and football' (Mac an Ghaill 1994, p.56), he identified a way to rise above the constraints of being a working-class sissy boy by aligning himself with smart middle-class kids. Struggling to perform and participate in cultural notions of working-class gendered heterosexuality where football, swearing and not being a 'swot' became the substance that facilitated enactments of male bonding (Connell, 1989), he displaced himself into a 'community of practice' (Paechter, 2003) where being a 'swot' was a preferable label than 'fat poof'. Finding a way through the difficulties of his youth meant finding a way to fit in with what was culturally and socially accepted, what constituted 'normal' patterns of behaviour. Being middle-class, he believed, distanced him from the expectations of 'The three Fs'; it allowed him to construct a masculine identity that was not being seen as unusual or suspicious. Literacy was central to that endeavour, to not only imagine another way of being but also to be seen as academic, an affiliation that made it easier to pass as straight.

Being seen to be clever and being seen to be middle-class was a camouflage for Mother's embodied sexuality and it offered a way out of being identified and stigmatised. It enabled him to pass, a useful tactic to overcome the difficulties of being a working-class, sissy-boy queer. Green (1998) has pointed out how there are not many rewards for integrating a stigmatised identity and that '...normative heterosexual behaviours are socially rewarded and transgressive behaviours are punished' (Green, 1998, p26). Paradoxically, reading offered a way of becoming less visible as gay in a community that valorised a strategic, essentialised construct of masculinity in which 'real boys' 'rejected the official three R's (reading, writing and arithmetic)' (Mac an Ghaill, 1994, p58). Real boys played football and they distanced themselves from the curriculum subjects and activities perceived as feminine (Paechter, 2003), such as enjoying reading literature or getting involved in drama productions. Masculine identities were apparently being produced through a perception of how certain curriculum subjects were regarded as gendered. In Mother's case, literacy was a way of displacing himself into a safer space that removed him from those attitudes.

> Mother: *I was in the top set and effectively had been ghettoised. There were 250 kids in my year and there were some fucking nutters but I was in a group of 30 and I stayed with those 30 right up to 'O' level. There were occasions, mainly for biology, when we were in a mixed ability class, when we joined with the nutters and at those times I always tried to keep a low profile, I stayed in the corner with my friends Penelope and Sophie and we got our heads down and worked. I was weird and Other and different and they knew it. Being in the top set ghetto made being queer easier. I was bright and that meant I could get awaywith stuff like reading, not liking sport and having friendships with girls.Texts and reading were escape. I became a voracious reader because I had cottoned on that the class thing was also a language thing. I took what I needed from literature to start changing myself.*

Masquerading as middle-class and passing as straight meant that throughout his adolescence and in relation to his schooled and other identities, Mother occupied a liminal space (Turner, 1977). A liminal space describes being in-between, not quite inside or outside. Mother was not quite middle-class, but had removed himself from his working-class family, not quite masculine enough yet not completely feminine, undecided if he was 100% gay but knowing that he wasn't 100% straight. It would seem that occupying such a space would be problematic, yet a liminal space can be productive, it can offer a location where transformations can happen. The experience of liminality can provide a means through which to adjust our perspective of ourselves and the world we in which we live. Turner (1977) has explained that 'if liminality is regarded as a time and place of withdrawal from normal modes of social action, it can be seen as potentially a period of scrutinisation of the central values or axioms of the culture in which it occurs' (Turner, 1977, p167).

Speaking about liminal spaces in relation to literacy, Schechner (1988) coined the term 'Creases' to describe the meeting point where the worlds of dominant and vernacular literacies converge. He suggested that they can become places in which to hide and, from Mother's account of reading, it was in the Creases that he initiated a symptomatic reading that recognises the presence of more than one discourse in a text and where meaning is generated by what a text does not say (Althusser, 1968). Hiding within the Creases of literacy activities became important for Mother so he could re-imagine, dream and fantasise about possible future lives. Fisher (2003) notes how 'daily practices developing from liminal spaces seem to be infused by a logic of more-than-oneness, a 'doing' of life that is inflected with multiple layers of narratives rather than any singular one' (Fisher, 2003, p174).

For Mother, stories were an escape route out of the everyday world of heterosexuality, a means through which he could explore the possibilities of another way of living a queer life. A Queer reading of texts might be thought of as one in which there are multiple attachments and identifactory indeterminacies that resist a heterosexual framework for understanding the self in the world and what one has to become. In Queer readings of texts it becomes possible to create opportunities for identities to proliferate and not merely represent. Martin (1996) speaks of the queer possibilities of identifying in this way and says that books 'produced the fantasies into which [she] escaped or imagined escaping the painful effects of the rules governing sexuality, gender and maturity' (p. 35). Thinking about how Mother was projecting himself beyond the immediate into a future of his own making in order to tell a different story of himself leads me to suggest that texts throughout his adolescence became a resource for reclaiming power and experiencing agency.

> Mother: *I couldn't wait to escape and reading was my lifeline to another place. I wasn't there and I wasn't seen as being real and therefore I got* Wuthering Heights. *I understood what and who Kathy was: Kathy was marginal and disempowered. Likewise, I too was waiting to escape from the turgid everyday swamp that was my life. I was reading those texts and it had everything to do with class and to do with being queer. I identified with the weak protagonist, with not having a voice, being invisible yet being present.*

Talburt suggests that queer youth 'dwell in two devalued positions relative to the binary categories heterosexual/ homosexual and adult/youth' (Talburt, 2004, p17), making it doubly difficult to experience agency. However if, as Appadurai (1996) has suggested, the imagination has a significant role to perform in social life, it might be in the identity work that gets done by the imagination.

> Mother: *From books and movies I was inventing another life. There are certain texts where you do lose yourself and that can be really dangerous 'cos then you have to look up and have to face the outside world.*

Adolescence is a time of many crossroads. Texts can offer a space to contemplate who we are and what we want to become. They can provide a meeting point between the outside everyday world and the interior knowledges we have of ourselves. Re-thinking reading as an activity in which identities can, over time, become known, displaced or reconfigured can mean that reading and texts are able to give a home to our passions, our dreams, our fears and our anxieties. It may be that through our imaginative endeavours we are best placed to consider the difficulties, pains, pleasures and needs of our lives (Measor and Sikes, 1992). Winterson (1991) has commented how:

> Everyone, at sometime in their life, must choose whether to stay with a ready-made world that may be safe but which is also limiting, or to push forward, often past the frontiers of common-sense, into a personal place, unknown and untried. (Winterson, 1991, pxiv)

What Mother said about how his involvement with books and movies became increasingly important as a means for resisting the practices of heteronormativity leads me to suggest that for many gay youth, their imaginative encounters with texts are central to experiencing agency (Appadurai, 1996).

Perhaps it is within their imaginative endeavours that they find themselves better placed to push beyond the difficulties of everyday life and imagine a better future for themselves.

Beyond the book, off the screen

> ... written words sounds like a pistol shot in many a closet. ...literature... and books ...have often served as the powerful tools of self knowledge and acceptance for generations of gay men and lesbians. (Escoffer, 1993, p 7)

Mother spoke about his future in a way that hinted at how texts were part of an on-going dialogue between the past, present and future. He described how, through texts, he summoned up the ability to sustain himself as a working-class sissy-boy and found the means to imagine a way out of challenging situations. Mother acknowledged how he felt split between the life he was living and the one he wanted to live, and how he found a way through adolescence by using texts to re-imagine the world and fantasise about possible future lives. He spoke about believing how, in the imagined future, another life could unfold. Mother became a protagonist in his explorations of identity, a process that involved considering plurality as opposed to singularity and there being a possibility of selves as opposed to a self (Dunkel and Anthis, 2001; Markus and Nurius, 1986).

Appadurai suggested that it is through the imagination that 'individuals... have found the space to refigure their social lives, live out proscribed emotional states and sensations' (Appadurai, 1996, p5). By exploring how the reader can have as much significance as the work of literary fiction in the reading encounter (Rosenblatt,1976), it becomes clear how Mother's sexuality shaped what he did with texts and how, once decolonised from heteronormative modes of meaning making, the figured world of the text was better positioned to acknowledge and reflect back a queer presence and engage with queer desire.

> Mother: It was rare that I would encounter a gay character or a gay text but I learnt how to flip stories to serve my own ends. I conjured gay subtexts up from out of nowhere because I had to...

If the course of identity development is dialogic, repetitive and occurs in the exchanges between the self and the social environment, then at some point during adolescence the influence of sexual desire will set the context for what texts are read and how they get read. Saint-Aubin (1992) observed how:

> ...the dynamics of sexuality and sexual object choice will influence how readers ascribe meaning to literary texts. In fact, although other aspects of

our identities come into play when we read, sexual identity is unique and central because of the role that it plays in the creation of subjectivity. (Saint – Aubin, 1992, p65)

Mother spoke at length about how his sexuality, even when he was very young, was a salient presence in his reading of texts and how his reading identity offered a form of pleasure, freedom and escape from the impossibility of living outside the infinite heterosexual narratives. Reading symptomatically was producing knowledge about experience(s) he had not yet lived.

Mother: *I remember the first time I saw the film* Seven Brides for Seven Brothers, *I loved the romanticism and I loved the kidnapping idea. I wanted to be kidnapped cos I knew I would get to be banged senseless in a log cabin by Howard Keel... Have you ever seen a film called* Tim, *with Mel Gibson? That was a biggy for me. I saw that as a teenager and cried my eyes out, wept buckets. It was a very heterosexual movie – he was this emotionally damaged, physically scarred solitary male figure and it was so sad. The only reason I throw that in is because straight people go, 'Ugh' and gay people go, 'Yeah, we got it'.*

I also remember seeing Interview with a Vampire, *when it first came out, with a group of straight friends and I will always remember talking about the sexual tension between the Brad Pitt and Tom Cruise characters, it was obvious, it was soooo obvious. It is deeply homoerotic, they almost kiss several times, it's like, for the love of god, wham your tongue down his throat, that's what we want to see. I use that as an example 'cos I saw it again two weeks ago and I hadn't seen it since I first saw it and, yeah, it is homoerotic, I was so surprised that the people I was with when I first saw it just didn't get it.*

More recently there has been The Lord of the Rings *trilogy and there is massive homoeroticism in it, all that, 'Oh let me carry you Mr Frodo, I will always be with you Mr Frodo', 'Oh, Mr Frodo, we can't go on any more.' Let's face it, they should have had a shag and got it over with. You know, we really wanted them to. He loves him, they are two huge poofs and then at the end one of them dies and the other one marries a curly haired woman and has two kids. Another example of queers being killed off or having to go straight for a happy ever after ending.*

In her transactional model of reader response, Rosenblatt (1976; 1978) outlined how the values and attitudes of the reader are influential in the reading encounter. She advocated that the relationship between text and reader is of primary importance in that the reader can have as much significance as the work of literary fiction (1976). Rosenblatt (1978) considered how the reader assumes an active role in the meaning-making process and spoke about how the reader undergoes a lived-through experience with a text. In foregrounding the reader's experience in relation to the text, she rejected traditional epistemology that considered literature to be a body of knowledge that could be appropriated and understood through critical instruction. Instead, she conceived of it as an encounter between the worlds of the self with the world of the text. Rosenblatt (1978) reinserted the reader into the reading process and redefined 'literary experience by emphasising the individuality of each reader and the inevitable uniqueness of each reading event' (Connell, 2000, p4).

Theorising a triadic relationship of text, reader and experience, a transactional model of reader response centralises the social project of reading. A response does not take place in a vacuum; it is involved with the reader's immediate social experience. Response is mediated by what is brought to the text so a transaction between an object (text) and a subject (reader) requires each to participate and be affected by the other. Rosenblatt, in her theory of reader response, moved the focus away from the privilege, authority and normative messages of the text afforded by an 'efferent' reading to the value of interpretative acts in an 'aesthetic' reading.

Rosenblatt (1978) used 'efferent reading' to describe what the reader wants to take away from the reading, a fact to remember. She used 'aesthetic reading' to describe an experience or identification that a reader wants to live through. Rosenblatt refused to separate out acts of interpretation from their social implications and argued that a transactional model provides a self-renewing framework for self realisation. An 'aesthetic reading' suggests how the reader can not only attend to 'what words point to in the external world...[but also] to the images, feelings, attitudes and associations and ideas that the words and their referents evoke' (Rosenblatt, 1978, p10). Such a stance makes it possible for the secret interior world of sexuality to be unfolded, become visible and be mapped onto and into the reading encounter. Reading, therefore, acts as an analogue for the act of knowing, a transformational process between reader and text – a knower and known – which frames experience in a social dimension. She noted how 'books are a means of getting outside the particular cultural group into which the individual was born' (p228) and articulated a process by which '...literature can play an important part in the process through which the individual becomes assimilated into the cultural pattern (p222) .

How Mother *flipped stories to serve* his *own ends* illustrates how a text may bring into play and be related to 'profoundly personal needs and preoccupations' (Rosenblatt,1976, p182). But it also shows how Mother's reading of texts were focused around meeting specific needs and desires. As Rosenblatt states in *Literature as Exploration*:

> Young people who encounter works of literature are building up their sense of the socially favoured types of adjustment in our culture. In books they are meeting extremely compelling images of life that will undoubtedly influence the crystallisation of their ultimate attitudes, either of acceptance or of rejection... Literary works offer... some approach to life, some image of people working at a common fate, or some assertion that certain kinds of experiences, certain modes of feeling are valuable. (Rosenblatt, 1976, p20)

Perhaps, then, texts can be considered as opening up a space in the lives of gay youth where they can begin to deconstruct the discourses surrounding gender and sexuality and start to speak back:

> Mother: *Relationship with texts became part of that significant passage from not knowing to knowing. What they did for me, at that time, was to push me towards realising that something was happening inside me that was different.*

Proliferating the practices of literacy

Gee (1990) and Scribner and Coles (1988) posit the idea that literacy is part of larger discourses, that it is a way of being and is constitutive of identity in terms of a subject being enculturated into social practices. Street (1984) and Barton (1994) have promoted the idea of literacy as being embedded in larger life practices and I have found it increasingly productive to speak of literacies rather than literacy to represent the diasporas of experiences and identities which are so often absent from our understanding of how texts are read and what they can come to mean in individual lives. I hope that in mapping a relatively uncharted terrain, and in investigating the socio-sexual contexts of literacy practices, that I have expanded an understanding of 'literacy not as singular or monolithic', and have contributed to an understanding of how literacy is '...variously embedded and situated within diverse institutional and cultural practices' (Rowan *et al*, 2002, p92).

Holland *et al* (2001) have noted how 'persons are now recognised to have perspectives on their cultural worlds that are likely to differ by gender and other markers of social position (Holland *et al*, 2001, p31). The extent to which these perspectives are recognised or embraced in our classrooms, especially in relation to sexuality, is largely determined by the efforts of individuals who dare to speak against the disciplining force of heteronormativity (Vicars, 2006).

Mother described how, through his adolescence, his relationship with texts was one that enabled him to pass, and distance himself from the regulatory framework of working-class masculinity. That he was able to construct from out of texts a way to disassemble identity, 'decenter centres and disrupt hierarchies' (Kamberelis, 2004, p167) meant that his use or, some might argue, abuse of texts became his way of queering the centre by centring the queer. As Hagood (2004) observes:

> If adults don't attend to adolescents' subjectivities and to adolescents' uses and constructions of text... and... If subjectivity is only seen as something that is dark and seditious, then adolescents' text uses can't be recognised as an attempt to push against and reshape the structures and identities that define them. (Hagood, 2004, p159)

If Mother's story can teach us anything, it is that youth who are questioning their sexuality or youth who have identified as being lesbian, gay or bisexual are positioned by the discourses and practices of heteronormativity in adolescence. Texts can offer a resist-stance to such attitudes and afford a means of working a way out of the constraints and limitations of being 'queer'. Britzman has suggested that 'while gay and lesbian youth are busily constructing their sexual identities, they always encounter contradictory and hostile representation of their identity work' (Britzman, 1997, p194). If this is so, texts offer a space for gay youth to imaginatively explore identity and can 'rearticulate received representations of heterosexuality with their own meanings' (Britzman, 1997, p 195).

Concluding remarks

> To be excluded from a literature that claims to define one's identity is to experience a peculiar form of powerlessness-not simply the powerlessness which derives from not seeing one's experience articulated... but more significantly the powerlessness which results from the endless division of self against self... (Fetterley, 1978, p xiii)

In seeking to illuminate the relationship between sexual identity and textual experience, I am reminded of Kerby's (1991) view that what we choose to name as the self, in terms of identity, is constantly being rewritten and is analogous to the act of reading. The potential of texts to generate greater understanding of who we are and what we want to become suggests that texts exist, like the self, in a temporal dimension and offer an interpretative location in which to re-perceive and reinterpret lived experiences in relation to the lives of fictional characters. It seems likely that reading became increasingly important to Mother for generating knowledge and understanding about his sexuality in ways that countered the heteronormative.

Unless we as teachers begin to realise that many of our students are reading between the lines, beyond the book and off the screen, and understand how and why such interpretations are being made, we risk failing to hear the diaspora of voices that energise texts. Unless we also open up our classrooms and our reading of texts to engage with students' worlds in which issues of sexuality are as salient as 'race' or gender, and unless we as educators engage with new methods and theories, language and interpretative lenses to recognise that literacy practices are embedded in wider discourses then, as the Scarecrow in *Wizard of Oz* (Metro-Goldwyn-Mayer, 1939) said, 'It's no use screaming at a time like this because nobody will hear you!'

7

BLENDING VOICES, BLENDING LEARNING: LESSONS IN PEDAGOGY FROM A POST-16 CLASSROOM

Julia Davies and Kate Pahl

How can exciting, innovative and inspirational inclusive teaching and learning be achieved in a post-16 subject English classroom? Strategies are currently being sought to engage disaffected 14-19 year-old learners in the literacy curriculum and sustain their interest (Bird and Akerman, 2005; Hamilton and Wilson, 2006). This chapter shows how this can be done. It describes an innovative project which responded to the interests and concerns of this age group and successfully supported the students through one course, which was used as a stepping stone to another. The project employed and valued texts from popular culture, using narratives and experiences from the lives of the young people on the course as part of the course itself. It used these resources in ways that allowed learners to analyse and understand popular texts in a new light, and gave them the literacy resources to deconstruct more traditional 'schooled' texts, such as those used in the GCSE curriculum. In the course of doing so, they were transformed into learners who engaged positively with the curriculum, its content, and with each other.

We were invited into the Young People Speak out (YPSO) programme, a 'blended learning' course, by its tutors, who requested our support as 'critical friends' in evaluating and developing their work. Part of the project was funded by the National Research and Development Centre (NRDC) as one of their practitioner research projects, aimed to encourage practitioners to research ways of finding and engaging new learners (Euseden and McCullough,

2006). Supporting the tutors, we also became involved in the research process, in evaluating the course and developing a theoretical framework which enabled us to investigate and consider why it worked so well.

The course tutorial team wanted to understand the processes at work in their classrooms. They had set up what they believed to be a successful programme, designed for students with 'low level literacy skills', who were not yet ready to follow the General Certificate of Secondary Education (GCSE) in English. The tutors wanted us to help them explore what made their course 'work for the students'. They noticed that normally reluctant students were staying with the programme, enjoying and engaging with the materials and making such good progress that they could move onto GCSE work the following year. Whilst the college tutors were aware of their institution's 'retention' targets, it soon became clear to us as researchers that this was a personal mission for tutors. We saw that they were keen to retain students on their courses because they believed education could help learners to lead fuller lives and they were keen to build on the 'funds of knowledge' (Moll, 2000; Gonzalez, Moll and Amanti, 2005) the students brought with them. They were able to develop a course which nurtured the students' expertise while offering them the analytical skills and knowledge that would deepen their understandings and broaden their perspectives of their own and others' lives.

The Young People Speak Out course was described to us as a pre-GCSE 'blended learning' programme. Whitelock and Jelfs (2003) identify three definitions of 'blended learning', while Oliver and Trigwell (2005) argue that there are many more versions than this and that the term is 'ill defined and inconsistently used' (Oliver and Trigwell, 2005: 24). It is therefore worth detailing the design of the YPSO pre-GCSE course. It was developed as an online resource as well producing fit for purpose, high quality printed materials which, as one tutor explained, looked 'more like a magazine'. Learning took place in a context where the tutor and the students engaged face-to-face in a range of tasks as a group, in pairs or individually, according to the judgement of the tutor or the choices of students. Students chose the materials, whether online or printed, and had access to them outside the classroom too. The content for the course, described below, was directly relevant to the students' lives and engaged with popular culture. The format was systematic, but the delivery was highly participatory, varied, inclusive and supportive.

Our principle theoretical tool was the concept of Third Space theory as described by Bhabha (1994), Moje *et al* (2004), Sheehy and Leander (2004) and Wilson (2000), which we consider to be a useful frame for understanding some of the complex processes in the creation of a collaboratively constructed learning space where teachers and students explored and created meanings together. We had examined how other researchers had documented the benefits of embedding popular culture in the curriculum (Alverman, Moon and Hagood, 1999; Dyson, 1997; Marsh and Millard, 2000), something the YPSO course depended on.

We were able to observe the ways in which pedagogical style, the course materials and their mode of presentation, helped create a fruitful shared space for learning. By describing the project and our involvement in it, we hope to contribute to ongoing discussions about learning in third spaces and to report on the work of innovatory practitioners. Offering a theoretical framework combined with a description of this inspiring and innovative pedagogy will, we hope, be of use to both researchers and practitioners.

We have drawn on several data sources collected between September 2004 and June 2005. Our regular meetings with the course team to discuss areas for *their* research agenda involved us in introducing theoretical concerns and developing a framework that we have also drawn upon here. Although the college team generated additional data by means of questionnaires and interviews with students, here we rely upon data drawn from the following:

- informal discussions with tutors and group meetings
- classroom observations, including:
  - language
  - use of space
  - wall displays
  - use of materials
  - student interaction
  - teaching approaches
- analysis of course materials
- informal discussions with students
- evaluation of a separate pilot project of YPSO in local schools (Davies, 2005)

Both researchers jointly observed the classroom sessions and amalgamated their field notes. These were organised according to Wollcott's system of interpretation and analysis (1994); our fieldnotes were arranged into three columns separating the descriptive, the analytical and the interpretative. Although such divisions are somewhat artificial and there were overlaps, we found this method useful in helping us to identify when our fieldnotes had moved into an analysing and interpreting mode, rather than simply noting down what happened or what we saw. The organised data were shared and discussed with the tutors in group reflective research sessions, so we were able to move beyond idiosyncratic interpretations and to acquire useful additional information about the field. Thus, Wolcott's system gave us an opportunity to consider the classroom observation in a variety of ways, provoking discussion and developing analysis.

From the project with the tutors, Julia Davies (2005) developed an evaluation of the way the course worked with local schools. The project with schools has given us further insights into how the success of the project connects with both the project materials and their teaching; it was clear that the success of YPSO involved both the content of the teaching and the teaching itself. The relationship between these two domains was crucial in the creation of a space where tutors and students could share equally – what could be described as a 'third space'. We were clear that whilst the content of the materials contributed to the creation of the third space, it also developed from the manner of teaching and how the teachers engaged with students through the materials. It was the relationship between the students, the tutors and the materials that enabled the development of a critical third space.

The Young People Speak Out (YPSO) course

This course was aimed at students who already felt themselves to have failed, even to *be* failures. Tutors reported to us that the students involved in YPSO had all initially applied to follow the one-year GCSE programme but had failed to reach the level required to be accepted onto it. We were told that the level of despondency at the beginning of any so-called pre-GCSE course is therefore likely to be high and such classes can be famously difficult to motivate and teach. One tutor spoke of the students like this:

> They often feel like failures from the start. These are the people who have failed at school, or failed to attend school; they come to us saddened that they have to take their GCSEs after the rest of their peers have done so – only to discover when they get here, that the time delay will be even longer. (Individual tutor interview, September 2004)

The course is mainly taken by full-time students aged seventeen to twenty who are also following vocational courses. We were told:

> The students are often disaffected with what they see as 'purely academic' subjects, ones which are so often required by employers but which do not

seem to relate to what they really want to do in their lives. (Individual tutor interview, September 2004)

The pre-GCSE students were perceived by the tutors as having certain diffi-culties:

- they had low confidence levels in their own ability and past achieve-ments
- they were disengaged from courses they saw as irrelevant generally and to their plans for the future, save as an academic requirement
- they felt a sense of dislocation from their peers who seemed to be mov-ing ahead of them in their life plans and academic achievement.

Many of the students had experienced challenging circumstances such as fleeing countries at war, homelessness, homophobia, and difficulties with parents. They carried much complex cultural knowledge with them, and they were interested in popular culture – fashion, music, agony columns and so on. The pre-GCSE English team sought to develop a course that valued stu-dents' cultural knowledge and their interests beyond the college and which might build up their self-esteem and confidence by providing them with a forum that would make them feel empowered. The resulting course was con-structed around popular culture, digital technologies and the local com-munity – featuring the lives of people who had attended the course in pre-vious years and of young celebrities who had made it against the odds. The young people were the experts in much of the project content, whilst the college tutors could give them the language and tools to articulate and refine their views and feelings on the content and help them analyse how popular cultural artefacts of poetry, song and fashions were such effective forms of expression. The requisite skills for the English GCSE were also embedded in this contemporary programme. The course content was clustered around three main themes:

- Home and Homelessness
- Music Media
- Rap and Poetry.

The teaching took place in a purpose-built college classroom with enough computers to allow each student to work individually. There was an inter-active whiteboard and in the centre was a cluster of tables, boardroom style, at which the students could sit and discuss issues in a plenary setting. The layout of the room, as will be discussed, was seen to facilitate a specific range of pedagogies. Because the course was delivered both on-line and through paper based materials, the students were offered a choice of modes to work within.

The full content of the course was accessible via a secure website, and each student's work could be stored in it online. The site was partly interactive and students could write directly into the teaching materials and undertake activities such as cloze or sequencing exercises. This resource was duplicated in the form of paper-based booklets which the students owned and could write in. Such flexibility gave them the choice of working online or on paper. The booklets which made up the paper-based version of the website materials were eye-catching, professionally produced and illustrated and the design and graphics resembled young people's magazines. The layout used varied types of text and fonts, and contemporary images of, for instance, rap artists and local young people (see Figure 7.1).

The flexibility of the media in which the students could choose to work, the contemporary style of the materials and their quality production, the topics covered and the overall multimodal approach all reflected the ways in which young people use and interact with media in their lives beyond the college.

Some of the resources included biographical texts produced by college students, quotations from students about a variety of issues, and photographs of past students. The materials included local references, thus valuing the students, their views and their interests and placing them at the heart of the YPSO course.

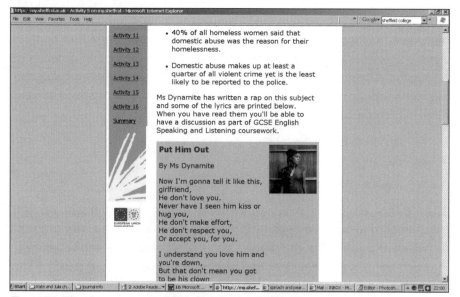

Figure 7.1: Sample course material to show layout and design.

Theoretical perspectives

One key aspect of the course, which we recorded in our observation notes, was how everyday literacies and 'funds of knowledge' from the students' experiences were occurring naturally in the classroom (Moll *et al*, 1992; Gonzalez, Moll and Amanti, 2005). For example, the break-time activities appeared to differ little in substance (content and modality) from the planned classroom activities, and in many ways looked exactly the same. When we first reported our observations to the tutor involved, she was very concerned lest her lessons had seemed directionless, poorly organised and 'uneducational'. However, our observation showed us that the students wished to continue working on the same resources, in the same manner, through their breaks as well as in lessons. This indicated that the course materials and the tutor had managed to create a classroom atmosphere which valued, yet subtly directed, the funds of knowledge the students had brought with them.

> During the break students stayed in and around the classroom, and used the computers for accessing emails and using the internet. Some had up Arabic websites and were looking at emails or doing other college work. (Classroom observation, February 26th 2004)

The students listened to CDs and looked again at the slideshow the teacher had used. They moved through a range of text types, engaging with the resources supplied by the course and those they had brought in. Dyson writes thus about how educational institutions work:

> ...to everything there is a time and place and, for the most part, school is not the place for popular culture. Popular culture though, is not so easily contained in physical time and space, and the reason for that has to do with 'people'. ... the history of popular culture has been tied up with efforts to distinguish between 'them' from 'us'. (Dyson, 2006, pp xvii-xviii)

Popular culture is not definable simply as a genre or form, such as radio programme, or as ballad or rap. It is moveable across domains and seeps into classroom spaces as text-makers construct texts and bring 'funds of knowledge' to the materials they engage with. It may be more to do with the *practices* that surround the materials, how they are used, when and by whom. Dyson draws on Jenkins (1992):

> In particular societal circumstances, people use whatever symbolic material is to hand to develop shared meaning making practices. That is people produce popular culture by participating actively in making use of cultural commodities ... They re-tell, role-play, shift genre, merge characters, on and on appropriating and recontextualising material from commercial texts as they participate in a shared community. (Dyson, 2006, p xviii)

Through such processes, identity can be explored, enacted, developed and drawn upon; the experiences are potentially rich and help individuals engage with each other in a range of ways. In the YPSO classroom these processes were developed through students engaging with materials and each other in a manner where they could be deemed as experts, experiment and move freely across texts.

It was important for both the course content and its delivery that students' experiences were brought into the classroom and built upon in class activities. For example, students described their experiences of migration, and this formed part of the reading material for the class.

Moje *et al* (2004) argue for the importance of acknowledging the different funds of knowledge from homes, peer groups and other systems and networks of relationships that young people draw on when they make meaning (Moje *et al*, 2004: 38). They argue that the socially created nature of these funds of knowledge, when brought into the classroom, help students recognise that the knowledge presented to them is also *socially* created (our emphasis) (p41). By placing a text from Eminem alongside a text from Blake, as the course materials do, different types of knowledge are placed alongside each other, and both are seen as equally valid. The texts are seen to draw on similar circumstances across time and space. Just as the young people were beginning to understand cultural diversity in terms of their own experiences

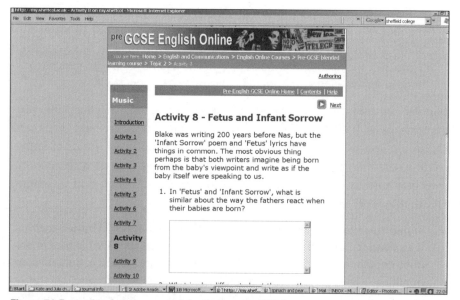

Figure 7.2 Example of course material – Eminem and Blake

and through the words of rap artists, they were able to observe it in 'classic literature' too.

As one student commented:

> I like Tupac. I love his rap. He sings for us. He is for us. For us young people. He wants us to be good, stay out of trouble. (Classroom observation field notes)

Third space theories have been increasingly useful for literacy researchers. Bhabha (1994) and Soja (1996) use the term to draw attention to how globalisation has increased the hybridity and blending people encounter in their oral and written texts. Bhaba focuses on the way in which third space is produced in and through language as part of sites of resistance. Likewise, Wilson identified the 'third spaces' of prison literacies, which were neither inside or outside the domains of prison or the outside world (Wilson, 2000). Soja (1996) argued more broadly for recognition of the spatial dimension of interaction, a point echoed by Leander and Sheehy (2004) and Blommaert, Collins and Slembrouck (2004) in their work on the spaces of multilingualism. The processes of creating third spaces however, have been less well documented. Moje and colleagues were among the first to describe and pinpoint how a third space can be constructed and maintained in the context of literacy learning, when they cited, for example, how young men's love of riding bikes, and in particular, stunt riding could be used to teach an understanding of risk, as well as concepts such as force and motion. Moje articulates why this activity was particularly relevant for the goal of developing third space, as it is a place of both resistance and knowledge (Moje *et al*, 2004:57). These kinds of cultural knowledge were similar to those drawn upon by the English on-line team: they were linked to peer activities and out-of-college contexts.

Here we focus particularly on teaching pedagogy as the mediator and constructor of the third space, as well as the materials. Taken together, these offer a radical teaching pedagogy which transforms disaffected students' opportunities for literacy learning, turning as this pedagogy does on the content of students' everyday lives and the recognition of their identities within the classroom in pedagogical interaction. When we watched the construction of this space, we also considered how it was constructed through the students' shared allegiances. We drew on Gee's notion of 'affinity spaces' (Gee, 2004) to describe the on-line and off-line spaces the students engaged with. These spaces could be brought together as a community of practice, for example, when the class group went to visit a rap artist as part of a concert programme.

They could be examined for signs of difference and similarity, for example when a Polish rap artist's music was brought into class. The affinity spaces within the class were discussed in groups and also explored online. Examples of these affinity spaces included:

- Bollywood musicals
- rap music
- concerns with gender and identity
- fashion
- popular culture
- agony aunt boards

These shared spaces were openly welcomed in the classroom, and the online spaces the students occupied as they followed the course materials and surfed the net melded with their affinity spaces. For example, the tutor took an interest in the worlds the students were exploring:

> Val (the tutor) asked Tina what she was doing on the emails, and Tina said she was giving advice to people on the message boards. (Classroom observation fieldnotes)

As students brought their experience into the classroom, it was made visible and discussed. The experiences of the students were seen as funds of knowledge, as here, when the tutor asked about the origins of rap music:

> Val (the tutor) asks, 'Where does rap music come from?'
>
> Leticia answers, 'Eminem used to hang out with black people and white people would bully him, that's why music – he is singing about too many angry white parents,' (Classroom observation fieldnotes)

Leticia went on to describe how Eminem was bullied at school in Philadelphia, and how black music was his refuge. She was drawing on her funds of knowledge as a black teenager engaging with issues of identity. Such is the nature of globalisation that Leticia was able to tell us that her cousin, in the country from which she had fled as a refugee, had loved rap. Her learning about rap not only gave her a way into the literacy curriculum at college but also helped her re-kindle familial connections in a way unanticipated by the course design. The crossing of global cultural boundaries of much popular culture allowed Leticia to make links across the different fields of her experience through the curriculum.

Gee's (1990) concept of Discourse, as describing people's ways of being, doing, acting, talking and dressing, is useful to pin-point how identity kits are visible in a number of different domains of communication. The classroom observations also focused on visible artefacts; we identified how the use of posters helped locate students' cultural worlds in the classroom:

> On the walls are images of male rappers, mostly revealing their underpants in a fashionable way above their trousers. Julia asks students about these (interested in the Muslim girls' views on such seeming immodesty). The students say they like them. There is a poster called 'Young People Speak Out' with images of students on the course at the back. There is also a display in the corridor. (Classroom observation fieldnotes)

The assemblage of images around the room brought together a range of cultures. This positioning visually reflected the diversity of cultures in the course materials and among the students themselves. An American magazine about rap lay on a table where the students worked; the computers often showed screens with Bollywood legends smiling out from screens; students' attire included track suits and jeans, studs in noses and gemstones on fingers and clothes signalled affiliations to religion (hijabs and burkhas). A diversity of students' Discourses was audible and visible during the teaching session; accents from the working class north of England combined with those from other languages and cultures. One student was encouraged to put on some rap music from Poland, her country of origin and the sound filled the classroom. As the rap unit was worked on, the tutor played rap tracks and the students listened, often thinking or working at the same time. The patterns of working the students engaged in were more akin to the way adults work, moving across domains, surfing the internet, chatting, reading visual images and listening to music. As one student observed:

> This is the only lesson where we can listen to music while we are working. It aids concentration! (Classroom observation fieldnotes)

We discussed how this way of working is familiar to us, as academics, who so often work at home, blurring the boundaries between leisure and work spaces and times, who might write, read, cook, blog, surf the internet, listen to music and compose emails, moving across these activities and spaces. This fluidity and seepage of one activity into another allows us to reflect on processes and to see connections that are often illuminating. Such messiness is seldom recognised as a positive working pattern in classrooms. It is regarded as disruptive to the boundaried curriculum with its timetable and schedule of demarcated activities. We argue that such an approach supports the creation of beneficial third spaces, allowing individuals to move across bounded Discourses. In this YPSO classroom, complex multi-tasking skills were celebrated:

> Girl behind [researcher] is on the Internet intermittently during lesson. This tolerated. She looks up a soap quiz, and Asian line. She flicks skilfully across windows... (Classroom observation fieldnotes)

But the girl was also working on the course materials, making progress and thinking across domains. Traditional signs of learning, which teachers often take for granted as necessary, were not focused on in this class; instead, students multi-tasked across modalities, their concentration not always obvious:

> G7 is engaged in the rhythm of the music as it plays, she nods her head showing engagement even though she is turned away from the group, e-mailing. (Classroom observation fieldnotes)

Such non-verbal forms of communication were acceptable in a learning environment that was fully multimodal and drew on the affordances of different modes – the internet, media, music, writing, speaking and listening – to deliver its curriculum (Kress 2003).

Identity and learning

At the heart of the course's success was the tutor's focus on the students' identities and a respect for their expertise. As Alvermann (2006) observes, many teenagers are disadvantaged by a discourse which places them in a position of 'lesser' when their expertise might well be greater than adults who teach them:

> I prefer, like Amit-Talai and Wulff (1995), to think of youth not as separate from the adult world but as 'knowing something else that has to do with their particular situation and surroundings' (p11). This situated perspective on youth culture argues for literacy practices that avoid categorising people in ways which divide us (the adults) from them (the youth). It also argues for exploring how all of us (adults and youth alike) act provisionally at particular times given particular circumstances and within particular discourses ... (Alvermann 2006:40)

This provisionality and complexity of role identities was evident in the class-room observations we carried out. The interaction between tutors and students can reflect this conundrum. In this excerpt from an observation, the tutor is negotiating the difficulty she has with official demands that the students need permission slips to attend a rap concert:

> There was a long discussion about the gig they were being invited to go to – firstly when, Monday or Tuesday. Val was very embarrassed as she said they had to bring in permission slips. Anne pointed out that this was like be-

ing a primary school child, and 'having slips in your lunchbox'. Leticia was outraged. She said, 'I have been 18 for two whole weeks and this happens'. The group went through all the things she could do now she was 18. Anne said she didn't even live at home. (Classroom observation fieldnotes)

Even in the more formal learning situations, the tutor's style was to let them think and reflect on the concepts. She would invite the students into the space of learning and ask for their opinion.

Conclusions

The course outlined in this chapter was successful for the following reasons:

- the teacher provided an open invitation to the students to reflect and to comment as they worked. The teacher did not construct herself as 'expert' but rather as joint partner in the enterprise

- the course involved the inscribing of students' identities into activities, texts and practices, whether through course materials, focusing on students' experiences and drawing on their writing, or through an open invitation to bring in music and artefacts from their out-of-college worlds

- the course relied on an unusual mixture of blended learning, switching across modalities to provide the students with a secure on-line platform and group interaction and exchange, using digital and paper-based materials

- the course reflected new working practices. The students were encouraged to browse the internet, email, go onto MSM, and listen to music while working. By honouring teenagers' home literacy practices, and recognising how technology encourages students to flip across domains, moving in and between landscapes of identity, the course opened out new learning possibilities. Learning was an open accessible activity, where negotiation of identities was both the subject matter and the space of practice.

These insights lead us to recommend greater openness to teenagers' habitual literacy practices. For example, these learners found listening to music while working helped their concentration. Multi-tasking across modes and domains, as it is done elsewhere, could be celebrated and incorporated into activities. The practice of texting or e-mailing while working could be incorporated into learning activities. Research which explores and celebrates new pedagogies includes the work of Cope and Kalantzis (2000); Alvermann (2006); Davies (2006b); Pahl and Rowsell (2005) and Larson and Marsh (2005).

These studies all feature examples whereby identities and cultural resources, including digital and multimodal resources, are inscribed into teaching and textual practices in schooled settings.

We hope that the classrooms of tomorrow will not be about control but about space, providing young people with 'third spaces' where different types of knowledge can freely mingle and be heard. Building on the work of Moje *et al* (2004), more examples could be provided of places that create third spaces. In this chapter, we have seen how online spaces provide a different kind of affordance for young people, one that they can freely control and manipulate, often helping the teacher with technical difficulties. Likewise, the use of popular culture such as rap music invites the students into an equal relationship with the teacher. This course: online, blended, engaged with contemporary cultural practices, is a model for engaging and inviting new learners into the classroom.

8

SOCIAL INCLUSION AND DIGITAL LITERACIES

Victoria Carrington

He who first shortened the labor of copyists by device of movable types was disbanding hired armies, and cashiering most kings and senates, and creating a whole new democratic world: he had invented the art of printing. (Thomas Carlyle, Sartor Resartus, 1833)

How do you know if you are socially included? If you *are* socially included you will see your values and practices reflected in mainstream culture as you move through the everyday. You will have avenues for participation in decision-making processes accessible to you and, in addition, have opportunities to engage with the political and economic life of the community in which you live. As you move across your neighbourhood, city and region you will find your own practices and values mirrored with easy familiarity in the tastes, styles and activities of those around you. To not experience social inclusion is to be rendered invisible – to lack access to important and powerful discourses; to be positioned as deficit; to be blocked from effective participation in the political and economic processes of the mainstream culture around you; and often, as a consequence to be spatially marginalised. Mandanipour *et al* (1998) take the view that social inclusion:

> is a multi-dimensional process, in which various forms of exclusion are combined: participation in decision making and political processes, access to employment and material resources, and integration into common cultural processes. (Mandanipour *et al*,1998, p22)

Thus any discussion of social inclusion has visibility and meaningful participation at the core. This chapter considers examples of visibility and participation in an era increasingly characterised by digital technologies and a growing need for digital literacies.

Introduction

In the late 20th century, Paolo Freire (Freire 1972; Freire and Macedo 1987) drew attention to the role of literacy in effective social participation. He argued strongly that literacy per se was not an automatic good but that it could work to either disempower or empower individuals and groups. As a consequence, it was his position that we each need the capacity and opportunity to 'read the word and the world' if we are to be empowered by the texts at our disposal, rather than at their mercy. Freire's message is unambiguous: literacy and texts and the ways in which they are made available via literacy instruction, are political issues where the fall-out is keenly felt in our daily lives, every day. Freire's message makes the connection between social inclusion and literacy clear: a key prerequisite for visibility and participation is the ability to 'read' the ways in which we are each positioned in the world by texts and literacy practices and to deploy and manipulate a range of texts and practices to bring about change.

For generations, the debates about participation and inclusion have understandably pivoted around print literacies, often manifesting in social engineering projects which have as a central component interventions about the ways in which printed texts are used in the home (e.g. *Sure Start* and its derivative *Bookstart* in the UK; *Head Start* in the USA). These interventions have been premised on the understanding that middle class practices with text – bedtime stories, environmental print, parent-child shared book experiences – would mediate what were considered deficit parenting practices and would, magically, result in higher cognitive development, educational achievement and a growth in social capital. Much of this pivoted on the cultural centrality given to particular practices with print text as a marker of educational and social mobility. However, in contemporary post-industrial nations such as the United Kingdom, Australia and Singapore as well as rapidly changing nations such as China and India, engagement with digital technologies has become a key social practice with strong associations with the production of, and access to, text, and powerful forms of participation and communication.

To be socially included increasingly involves the capacity to demonstrate ownership and use of a range of digital technologies ranging from mobile phones to computers and the internet. Digital technology has become so embedded in our society that we often manage not to see it. Gere (2002) argues that:

> We are beginning to cease to notice its presence and how it affects us, or at least take these aspects for granted. We sit in front of our computers at work, surf the net, send e-mails, play games on consoles, watch television that is both produced and, increasing, distributed digitally, read magazines and books all of which have been produced on computers, travel with our laptops, enter information into palmtops, talk on our digital mobile phones, listen to CDs or MP3s, watch films that have been post-processed digitally, drive cars embedded with micro-chips, wash our clothes in digitally programmable machines, pay for our shopping by debit cards connected to digital networks, and allow the supermarkets to know our shopping habits through loyalty cards using the same networks, withdraw cash from automatic telling machines, and so on. Digital technology's ubiquity and its increasing invisibility have the effect of making it appear almost natural. (Gere, 2002, p198)

This invisibility must be profound for children and adolescents who have no cultural or personal memory of the pre-digital era. For these young people, digital technologies are as unremarkable and ubiquitous as electricity was for our generation, becoming visible only in their absence. Recognising the importance of digital technologies and the practices that accompany them, the Council of the European Union has called on members to promote digital literacy as 'an element for full participation in society' (October 2001). The New Zealand government has recently defined digital literacy as 'the ability to use digital technology, communication tools or networks to locate, evaluate, use and create information' (http://www.digitalstrategy.govt.nz/templates/ Page 60.aspx, accessed 14th January 2005). From the perspective of contemporary literacy education, 'digital literacies' refers to the repertoires of skills and knowledge necessary to access, produce and understand text in a range of social contexts using an array of digital technologies. It also encompasses notions of audience, purpose and distribution.

Earlier, I noted that to be socially included means that you see your own cultural practices and values reflected in the dominant culture. There can be no clearer indication of who and what are included in mainstream culture than the toys it produces and markets for children.

Visibility in mainstream culture: Digital toys

Toys: so familiar, so easy to overlook, but such clear windows into the key narratives, practices and values of a cultural group. Social inclusion in a digital world begins here in childhood. From birth, the children in our society are embedded in a world of toys and consumer and popular culture that indelibly stamps the importance of digital technologies. Without mentioning the digital technologies embedded in a washing machine or family car, a visit to the local toy store-online or down the street is enough to demonstrate the high cultural value attached to digital technology. A simple key word search: 'laptops' on the Amazon online toy store yielded nineteen results. The list included the Lil' Bratz Luscious Lil' Laptop, the Small World Express Preschool Laptop, the Barbie 'Chat with me' Online Laptop, the Learning Journey Phonics Laptop, and the Oregon Scientific's Batman Power Wing Laptop and Hot Wheels Accelerator Laptop 5.0. While each laptop is stamped with a fascia that links it to an entire range of merchandising, movies and television series, there are clear indicators of what is considered crucial and worthy of 'teaching' the young. Each laptop is hinge closing and portable; each has an inset qwerty keyboard and a track-pad; each has a screen. The one feature that sets these toys apart from the real thing (although I am not sure that the term 'real' is correct here) is a screen size that is relatively small in comparison to 'real' laptops. The screen may be small, but it still functions in what appears to be the same way as 'real' laptops – the child keyboards and the letters and words appear on-screen; the child backspaces or highlights and deletes, and the letters and words disappear. While some toy laptops, such as the Learning Journey Phonics Laptop, have a more limited focus on pre-reading activities and phonics skill and drill, others include approximations of voice functionality and a range of pre-loaded activities and games that parallel those found on computers and laptops.

The sheer number of these toy laptops, some of them targeted at children as young as three, and their close approximation of many of the features and functionality of real laptops indicates their potency as cultural symbols, pedagogic tools and consumer items. Each toy is a pedagogic instrument using keyboarding, track-pads and often computer mice; about highlighting and deleting text; and about the terms associated with laptops use such as 'screen', 'keyboard', 'mouse', 'return', 'delete', 'space bar'. The toys enable children to play and model the use of these technologies and the discourses associated with them in an apprenticeship into 'adult' culture. Importantly, the laptops are not isolated. They share the toy aisles with the likes of the Barbie Wireless Camcorder and Barbie Desktop Computer, along with a range of portable DVD players and music mixers. This is the same list and mix of digital technologies that children and families shop for in electronic stores and have in their homes: they look the same, display the same lists of functionality and key discourses and, in so doing, demonstrate the types of knowledge, consumption patterns and behaviours with technology children will be rewarded for demonstrating in the future. At the same time children depicted on television, in books and in movies have digital technologies in their rooms and computers, mobile phones and the internet often feature as key plot mechanisms. A key to the plot resolution in *Jurassic Park* (1993) was the ability of a pre-adolescent girl to reboot the theme park's computer system; *Spy Kids* (2001) was premised on the ability of two children to use an armory of sophisticated digital 'spy' technologies to rescue their parents and save the world. This reflects the relevance of these technologies in children's lives: 85% of 9-19 years olds in the United Kingdom are daily or weekly users of the internet; one in three children aged five to nine owns a mobile phone (Nesta Futurelab, 2005). The clear message circulating across and through mainstream culture is that the ability to access and use digital technologies is an avenue to participation and social inclusion.

Amongst the toy digital technologies on display the mobile phone must rate esteemed elder status, not least because it has acquired a new position within children's culture. While very young children continue to be given toy versions of mobile phones, often branded with well-known children's tele-vision characters, they are soon given operating, fully networked phones. In the UK, the average age of first phone ownership is eight and the total phone ownership is 60 million, cutting across age, gender, class and cultural boun-daries. This is a strong indication of how deeply mobile phone technology has become embedded in the everyday practices of our culture.

From early brick-like and heavy models – all in early Model-T Ford black – mobiles have evolved into a truly mobile and personalised digital technology available in a rainforest of styles, colours, accessories and shapes – a tech-nology that has significantly affected the practices of everyday social (see Ito, Okabe and Matsuda, 2005) and economic life (Hermida, 2002). As part of this diversification and embedding into the everyday, phones are now designed specifically for children. The MYMO phone, released onto the UK market in late 2005, is limited to five phone numbers with three key buttons to press in order to dial those numbers, but comes in a range of colours, is moulded to look like a cat's face (complete with ears), and has a headset that is also used as a necklace. Giving replicas of this technology to children as toys marks their cultural value; its movement out of toy status into targeted technology demonstrates the movement of this technology into the everyday of social practice.

Toys are directly linked to ways in which individuals and groups learn to value and access the key narratives and practices of their society and culture. That so many narratives now revolve around digital technologies is telling. The emerging cultural pattern concerning toys suggests that for today's children, social inclusion will increasingly involve a range of capacities linked to access and use of digital technologies. Already, young children are prepared for a future of keyboarding in various guises: laptops, mobile phones and desktop computers. They are positioned as screen readers and writers, as capable technology users. This has relevance for the practices associated with literacy. Not long ago, children were given blackboards and chalk – replaced more recently with whiteboards and whiteboard markers – plus books and novels to be shared with adults, and activity books with pre-reading and pre-writing activities to be completed with pencils and crayons. These artefacts signified the importance of the technologies of print literacy – pen, paper, book. They also took as a given the role of the adult mediator of text and literate practices. Books were to be shared with an adult, often in an intimate one-on-one setting – a socially privileged moment of cultural transmission. While these items are still given, received, valued and used, young children were more likely to receive DVDs at Christmas 2005, personal music players, a 'toy' computer or a mobile phone as a primary gift. In 2005 the best selling toy was Character Option's Roboraptor; in 2004 it was Robosapien. The fastest growing toy category in 2005 was robotic and interactive games; the top-selling toy of 2005 was the Bandai Tamagotchi Connexion (British Toy and Hobby Association, 2006).

Importantly, if toys are a window to the value and practices of mainstream culture, then the view through the window is of digital technologies. Social inclusion and meaningful participation are increasingly likely to pivot upon consuming these technologies and producing texts and social practices using them.

Participation: Citizen reporting via digital technologies
When the Tsunami devastated the coastlines of Thailand, Indonesia and a range of other nations in 2004, it was 'amateur' footage from camera phones, digital video and digital cameras that first transmitted the tragedy to the world. During the Buncefield oil depot fire In December 2005, the BBC received 6500 e-mailed photos and video clips captured on mobile technology (Twist, 2006). Passers-by and purposeful spectators used their mobile phone cameras and videos to take eyewitness images, some out of personal interest, others in the hope of capturing something important, newsworthy and perhaps profitable. At the same time, text messages were sent via mobile phone to news outlets and between members of the public, acting to disseminate first-hand information and opinion to vast numbers of people rapidly and effectively.

Citizen reporting, also known as citizen journalism, caught the full attention of the mainstream media and moved into public discourse as images captured and transmitted via mobile phone were published in the aftermath of the July 7, 2005 London bombing. On that one day, the BBC received 20,000 e-mails, 3,000 images, 1000 e-mail video and stills and 3,000 text messages from the public (BBC, 2005). User generated content entered the mainstream. The most widely distributed of these was an image of commuters finding their way out of the London underground railway system, silhouetted against thick smoke, haze and debris. This one image became instantly iconic (voted one of *Time* magazine's Best Photos of the Year for 2005) and grass-roots citizen reporting as a new form of civic participation was born. Bowman and Willis (2003) have defined citizen journalism as:

> The act of a citizen, or group of citizens, playing an active role in the process of collecting, reporting, analysing and disseminating news and information. The intent of this participation is to provide independent, reliable, accurate, wide-ranging and relevant information that a democracy requires. (Bowman and Willis, 2003, p9)

The notion of commentary, dissemination of information and participation by the ordinary individual has been extended by the growth in weblogs and of blogging as an activity. According to *Wikipedia*, the online encyclopedia, a *blog*

> ... is a website in which items are posted on a regular basis and displayed in reverse chronological order. The term blog is a shortened form of weblog or web log. Authoring a blog, maintaining a blog or adding an article to an existing blog is called 'blogging'....A blog comprises hypertext, images, and links (to other web pages and to video, audio and other files) (http://en.wiki pedia.org/wiki/Blogs Accessed 4th February 2006).

Mobile phone ownership and use is endemic. Technorati (Technorati.com), a search engine which tracks weblogs, currently lists almost 30 million of them around the world and is adding up to 40,000 new blogs to its listings every day (Blogcount.com Accessed 1st February 2006). More startling still, the *Blog Herald* suggests that almost 100 million blogs have been created around the world (www.blogherald.com/2005/10/10). Young and old from places as diverse as Australia, China, Iraq, Iran Russia, Croatia, Malaysia and the United Kingdom blog, and blog in vast numbers. Not long ago blogs were accessed and produced only via software developed for use on computers. Recently, in response to the exponential growth in camera phone use and the desire to upload images quickly and effectively, mobile phone software has evolved to allow the development of what is now called moblogging (mobile blogging).

Mobile phone and computer have conjoined in the production of particular kinds of texts and social practices.

Each blog is set up using relatively standard software but can be customised so there are any number of different types of blog online, ranging from personalised diaries to news commentary and reporting to aggregates of niche items. Regardless of style or genre or mode of uploading information, each blog is a piece of digital text that requires bloggers to access and master a range of skills and knowledges to use the technology to produce text for particular socially oriented purposes. And text is *always* produced in and for a social context regardless of the technology. The particular affordances of digital technologies, however, produce texts that are dynamic and multimodal, rich with interconnections and mixed media. They can be disseminated instantaneously to a mass audience. They act as a link in the development and maintenance of communities of interest that form locally and/or globally. This influences the ability of individuals and groups to understand themselves as active participants in local and worldwide events and issues with a legitimate voice in public forums.

Other digitally supported forums for citizen participation and journalism have emerged alongside blogs. In South Korea, the online newspaper *Ohmy-News* (http://www.ohmynews.com/) is collaboratively created by 26,000 registered citizen journalists who provide around 80% of the daily news and editorial content. *OhmyNews's* editor and founder, Oh Yeon-ho describes the role of citizen journalism:

> With OhmyNews, we wanted to say goodbye to 20th-century journalism where people only saw things through the eyes of the mainstream, conservative media. The main concept is that every citizen can be a reporter. A reporter is one who has the news and who is trying to inform others. (cited in Bowman and Willis 2003, p12)

Other citizen journalist sites include peer-to-peer applications such as texting, newsgroups, wikis, chatrooms, and online forums. The online encyclopedia, *Wikipedia* (wikipedia.org), is collaboratively written and abridged, constantly evolving with no definitive, final version. The key aspect of this new form of participation is that it is just that – participative, dynamic and interactive. Information is no longer collected, weighted, reshaped, finalised and forwarded from a central mainstream news outlet. Instead, information is increasingly understood to be contingent and gathered, considered and disseminated through a range of media and to a range of audiences who will respond and interact, often updating and editing information as it passes by.

And as digital technologies are accessible to the young as well as to adults, the patterns of information access and production are also shifting. This is significant. Postman (1994) suggested that the control of information was a key mechanism in the construction of the modern 'childhood'. The capacity of young people to circumvent adult control and mediation of information is a shift which has wide-ranging implications. This bottom-up, interactive approach to information allows local issues and concerns to reach an audience. It provides opportunities to gather information from a range of sources and, just as importantly, to contribute and comment.

Conclusion: Social inclusion, citizenship and digital literacies

Benedict Anderson (1991) wrote of the colonising power of print and its role in the formation of the 'imagined communities' underpinning the emergence of the modern nation state. He wrote about the development of modern nationalism, noting that the simultaneity evoked by printed text allowed groups of people to 'imagine' themselves connected around ideas, beliefs and practices even if they were separated spatially. Anderson suggests that print-capitalism 'made it possible for rapidly growing numbers of people to think about themselves, and to relate themselves to others, in profoundly new ways' (p36).

The affordances of print were linked to the construction and representation of particular kinds of 'citizen' that in their turn connect to still powerful patterns of inclusion and exclusion. These citizens wrote and read themselves into existence in particular kinds of ways (and not others) linked to the manner in which print was created, stored and distributed, but also to how information is accessed and used. The ways in which individuals and groups imagine themselves in the contemporary context cannot, as Anderson suggested, be dislocated from the types of text produced and accessed, nor from the flows of information that circulate. As the mainstream increasingly pivots on the use of digital technologies, the types of text produced and distributed will become increasingly digital, reflecting and drawing upon the array of affordances which characterise them. Blogs are a useful example: creating a blog requires that the blogger deploy a range of skills to build a 'page' and to embed hyperlinks, images and audio; simultaneously the same blogger is working through issues of audience, mixing and blending a range of media, and choosing the appropriate tone and content via the selection and positioning of words, pictures, audio and graphics. The text that emerges has been carefully crafted out of the quite specific capacities of particular technologies to suit the social needs of its creator. The set of affordances made available allows the creator of this piece of text to link to a range of other texts, to engage in an ongoing interaction with other bloggers and, importantly, to access and to disseminate information to a potentially massive audience.

Where does all this leave the notion of digital literacy? The reach of digital technologies into our everyday lives is so extensive that children's toys are providing early pedagogic moments and our social practices are shifting. Consequently, to be socially included it is increasingly necessary to have the skills and knowledge to create and critique digital texts as well as to access them. This includes, but goes beyond, entry-level technological skills such as how to create a new document in a word processing programme, use a search engine, and download software. While it is necessary to be able to access and utilise digital technologies, it is just as necessary to be able to manipulate multimodal texts for a range of purposes and to navigate effectively through digitally created and linked links. In an era when information has become more accessible and where the barriers to dissemination are lowered, it is vital that the young are prepared appropriately.

Digital texts, by their very nature, link to different identities, to different outlays of skills and knowledge, to different patterns around authorship and different relationships with information. Whether or not they mimic the appearance of print text – and often they do – they are created via quite distinct technologies and are linked to emerging forms of participation and collaboration around text. They are also, whether we like it or not, linked to the politics of literacy. Paolo Freire maintained that literacy was about 'reading the world' as well as the word, but he argued also that we should adopt a view of literacy as cultural politics (Freire and Macedo, 1987). In this view literacy, never neutral or disconnected, is a set of social practices associated with technologies of print. Access to, or exclusion from, these practices is used to empower or disempower people, and Freire was encouraging individuals and groups to develop what David Byrne (2005) has called a 'political identity', understanding literacy as both a symptom and as a tool for action. We should remember that the political processes that swirl around literacy and literacy teaching do not disappear just because we are now making use of new technologies. We should also remember that teaching, in this view, becomes an innately political activity. Tyner writes that literacy in the contemporary digital age should be understood as:

> the ability to decode information in a variety of forms, analogous to the reading of print, but also applicable to audio, graphics, and the moving image, a process that Paolo Freire and Donaldo Macdeo call 'reading the world'. If citi-

zens can also manipulate and understand the processes to create messages and distribute them, that is 'writing the world,' then literacy practices accrue maximum benefit to the individual. (Tyner, 1998, p4)

This is the purpose of literacy: to 'accrue maximum benefit to the individual' and through her/him, the broader community. This is also the essence of social inclusion – the right, the opportunity, and the skills with which to participate and transform one's life path.

If teaching is a political activity, the emergence of new digital texts and practices around the affordances of new technologies presents challenges and opportunities to educators. School-based literacy instruction does not sit outside the cultural politics of literacy and has long contributed to differing outcomes and differentiated opportunities, which reduce some students' options. We must recognise our own complicity as educators in this process and make every effort to ensure that our classroom practices reflect the literacies our students will need in order to optimise their opportunities for effective and successful participation in their communities. Importantly, we must not allow ourselves to mistake enhanced access for effective inclusion. While we should argue that adequate access to a range of digital technologies should be a first principle, we must recognise that there is no simplistic linear relationship between number of computers and enabling inclusion. Inclusion in a digital society is about using the rich mix of digital technologies and the texts created with them in ways that enable effective participation – a recognition that should move us rapidly beyond counting numbers of computers and whiteboards per child per classroom and requires that, as a profession, we engage substantively with the broader issues around literacy and inclusion.

Because literacy practices have the potential to empower or to disempower, we have a responsibility to ensure that all children have opportunities to engage creatively and authentically with the array of affordances attached to a broad range of digital technologies to create dynamic and purposeful texts. To this end, we must scrutinise all new curricula and work to revise the old, to ensure that digital texts share a central place with print and are not used merely as hooks to traditional patterns and outcomes. Further, we must ensure that students have ample opportunity to develop and hone attitudes and skills to enable them to not just see and read the world using digital tools and texts, but ethically and effectively to challenge and change that world. But above all, we must not allow ourselves to be distracted from a clear and constant awareness of the purpose and potential of literacy, nor from the recognition that the teaching of literacy is, and always has been, a political activity with profound consequences for the children in our classrooms. It is when we forget this that we begin to fail our students.

Note

This article mentions several products that are proprietary trademarks or registered names. The symbols ™ and ® have been omitted for ease of reading.

9

ASSEMBLING DYNAMIC REPERTOIRES OF LITERATE PRACTICES: TEACHING THAT MAKES A DIFFERENCE

Barbara Comber

Introduction

Internationally new forms of advantage and disadvantage, exclusion and inclusion are being created by global economies and mobile worker populations which affect the lives of the children of the poor and their educational trajectories. Places are being re-made. The new geographical divisions are often on racial and class lines, with unequal resources for the education of the poor, the well-off and the wealthy. Despite these stark differences, many governments are insisting on normative standards and on mandated literacy programmes, which often emphasise 'the basics' and a return to the study of the literary canon. Michael Apple describes the combined effect of such changes as 'legitimating educational inequalities in conservative times'. It has produced 'even more educational apartheid, not less' (Apple, 2005, p274) and despite the rhetoric of choice we can be sure the poor will continue to be educated in what he describes as 'underfunded and decaying schools' (Apple, 2005, p287).

In many places the poorest populations find themselves in edge cities or rural and regional towns, as public housing is re-claimed and demolished as part of the urban renewal and gentrification of cities (Hull and James, in press; Lipman, 2005). Neighbourhoods are already material instantiations of inclusions and exclusions. At the time of these significant economic, employment and housing changes, there are wholesale demographic shifts in the educational workforce as many of the baby boomer generation prepare to retire and a new workforce is recruited and inducted into the teaching profession. This is a challenge in its own right at a time when the status and work conditions of teachers in many western post-industrial nations is declining. Recruiting and retaining teachers in 'hard-to-staff' school districts is a major challenge (Wilson *et al*, 2004).

Despite significant theoretical and policy moves in literacy education that acknowledge the complexity and plurality of literacy practices, internationally what constitutes classroom literacy is frequently colonised by standardised testing and scripted programmes. In the face of unrelenting media and political criticism of state schooling, some teachers are merely going through the motions, following lesson routines and activities which require little or no intellectual engagement for them or their students (Comber and Nichols, 2004). Worryingly, while the standards rhetoric promises improved outcomes, very often in schools in high poverty locations, the pedagogy is impoverished. At such a time, we need as a profession to re-invent school literacies and in so doing to make use of the whole breadth of the curriculum and beyond the limits of classroom walls. In order to do this we need to work with front-line teachers in knowledge-producing schools (Bigum, 2004). We need to produce, with young people, literacies with currency and durability – identity-shifting literacies, literacies with substantive consequences. This is not easy to achieve as many researchers have noted a pervasive deficit discourse often limits what is attempted and achieved in schools serving poorer populations (Comber and Kamler, 2004; Gonzalez *et al*, 2005; Gregory and Williams, 2000; Luke, 1998).

This chapter considers how teachers can make a difference to the kinds of literacy young people take up. Increasingly, researchers and policy-makers see literacy as an ensemble of socio-cultural situated practices rather than as a unitary skill. Accordingly, the differences in what young people come to do with literacy, in and out of school, confront us more directly. If literacy development involves assembling dynamic repertoires of practices, it is crucial to consider: what different groups of children growing up and going to school in different places have access to and make investments in over time; the kinds of literate communities from which some are excluded or included; and how educators make a difference to the kinds of literate trajectories and identities young people put together.

How teachers who work in schools in poor communities grapple with the politics of difference, social justice and critical literacy is my particular focus.

I am interested in the ways inclusive literacy practices are designed by particular teachers in particular schools in particular places and whether certain principles can be deduced from pockets of radical and innovative pedagogies. I ask:

- What can we learn from pockets of re-designed pedagogies, where literacy curriculum is not stripped to simulation by its school context?

- How is it possible to broaden and sustain radical inclusive teaching in times of increased stipulation of a dominant literacy?

As Apple (2005, p288) points out, 'most counter-hegemonic work is organised locally or regionally' and in neo-conservative times, radical social and educational movements have less capacity to mobilise alliances and be heard. So the documentating and disseminating of alternative enabling approaches to literacy education in high poverty and multicultural communities is crucial (see Comber and Kamler, 2005; Comber *et al*, in press; Dyson, 2003; Gregory and Williams, 2000; Kamler and Comber, 2005; Gonzalez, Moll and Amanti, 2005; Pahl and Rowsell, 2005, Vasquez, 2004). Such counter-hegemonic storytelling is important because many of the stories told about families living in poverty and indeed about schools in such communities are 'texts of terror' (Rappaport, 2000) – dominant cultural narratives – which demonise the poor and certain ethnic groups. What is needed are 'optimistic narratives' that reposition children and teachers as positive agents, as people who can make a difference.

> We cannot remake the world through schooling but we can instantiate a vision through pedagogy that creates in microcosm a transformed set of relationships and possibilities for social futures; a vision that is lived in schools. (New London Group, 1996, p19).

The New London Group's challenge is central to much of the collaborative research we do with teachers on critical and inclusive literacies. It's the 'transformed set of relationships and possibilities for social futures' (New London Group, 1996, p19) on which I focus. The examples which follow indicate how teachers' literacy pedagogy ensures that children have opportunities to assemble literate repertoires with currency, durability and consequences. Literacies with *currency* are practices which have exchange value in contemporary times; they are recognised as 'legal tender' across various sites of everyday life, in home, peer and school communities. I use *durability* in the sense defined by Brandt and Clinton (2002), who argue that there is a 'thingness' to literacy, something that can be taken from situation to situation beyond the local. Drawing on several recent projects which explicitly make space for teacher and student innovation, critique and creativity, I explore how literacy curricula can allow young people to assemble literacies with durability and currency, literacies with consequences.

Urban renewal from the inside-out

For over a decade my colleagues and I have enjoyed positive relationships with teachers and school leaders in the northern and western suburbs of Adelaide, Australia. Through a variety of media we have represented their explicit innovative work for social justice (Comber and Nixon, 1999, 2005; Comber *et al*, 2001; Nixon and Comber, 1995, 2005). The project explored here, 'Urban renewal from the inside-out', emerged from that history of close collaboration[i]. The school is in 'Westwood' – a precinct which was part of a vast area of the inner western suburbs of Adelaide slated for urban redevelopment. So public housing stock, the major source of cheap rental accommodation for low income earners, is being demolished. The new houses are marketed towards first home buyers, seeking relatively cheap accommodation close to the city and entry into the home ownership market. Few of the families who live in the rented public housing can afford to buy the new houses. Typically, they are offered alternative equivalent housing as 'nearby' as possible. Families and especially children have little opportunity to voice concerns about the effects of the redevelopment and many are positioned as passive observers of improvements that are being made for other people's children to enjoy.

We are committed to projects and practices that challenge such positioning and offer new possibilities and investments for young people in the life of the school. The staff of Ridley Grove Primary School had for some time wanted to enhance their relations with the preschool and the local community and to develop the school grounds and streetscape. These different interests were brought to bear in the 'Urban renewal from the inside-out' project, where children, teachers and educational researchers work with university architecture students and academics to re-design a part of the school grounds adjoining the preschool[ii]. We aimed to expand the range of literacies on offer to the children. We were curious about whether and how the children might explore and take up the spatial literacies offered by the architects. While we recognise that bringing out-of-school literacies into the place of school is not a simple matter (Hull and Schultz, 2001; Schultz, 2002; Sheehy, 2005), we believe that giving children access to the kinds of knowledges and discursive practices associated with urban redevelopment was potentially both motivating and politically ethical. Yet we understand the limits of schools as institutions and their capacities to 'school' authentic learning and doing practices, and unwittingly strip out meaning-making repertoires. Certain domains of literate practices may be more relevant to incorporate into a school's curriculum at different times and in different places. The literacies associated with journalism and architecture seemed particularly pertinent at this time and in this place. The Parks, the area in which the school is located, continued to be demonised in the local press, with headlines such as 'Residents living in fear of the neighbours'(Kelton, *The Advertiser*, 30th November, 2004). The children were witnessing the demolition of old housing, pavements and public spaces and the erection of new dwellings and services. We sought to induct children into the processes of recording change from their own viewpoints and also contribute to how a place might be re-made.

The university research team worked with the school principal and two teachers to build curriculum, with an emphasis on literacy but also on integrated elements of numeracy, science and the arts, around the design, negotiation and construction of the Grove Gardens. Academics from architecture, journalism and education allowed participating students from their faculties to negotiate their workload and assignments to take account of their contributions to the school garden. Children in Ruth Trimboli's Year Five/Six classes and Marg Wells Year Three/Four classes worked over two years with architecture, journalism and education students and academics to design and construct the garden. At the time of writing all structures are in place: the shade structures, the seating, the children's artworks, the paving and the rocky dry creek bed. What remains is the final researching and planting of the trees, shrubs and ground cover.[iii] The chapter next describes the literate practices children had the opportunities to assemble through their engagement in the project.

Critical and spatial literacies

Critical literacy includes deconstructive analytical language work but it can also involve students examining local realities, mobilising their knowledges and practices and designing and producing texts with political and social intent and real-world use (Comber, 2001, p276). It was these productive action-oriented characteristics of critical literacy that we sought to develop in this project, as well as what the architects described as 'spatial literacies' – ways of reading, designing and representing places to which people belong. Architect and academic Stephen Loo began with an illustrated PowerPoint presentation of unusual buildings, structures and places from various places and cultures around the world, to introduce the children in Wells' and Trimboli's classes to some key concepts and vocabulary associated with architecture, such as: design, community belonging, abattoir, asylum, spiral, beam. Later, he would explain specific structural elements such as platforms, walls and so on. Importantly, the children were hearing the vocabularies and discursive practices of architecture from the start. They were encouraged to imagine and consider unfamiliar worlds and structures even as they considered the mundane everyday spaces around them. Loo's presentation was followed by a visit to a working architectural studio at the university where the first year architecture students and Ridley Grove Primary School pupils participated in a workshop together.

For many years, the teacher, Marg Wells has worked with children researching their neighbourhood – places they go, places they don't, places they fear, places they enjoy, changes that were visible, changes on the drawing board, improvements that could be made and so on (Comber *et al*, 2001; Comber and Nixon, 2005). Thus she built her critical literacy curriculum around the neighbourhood in important ways. She made a critical analysis of local problems with the children and at the same time re-positioned them as researchers and citizens who could act on and in their community. So she brought a history of working critically and materially to the Grove Gardens project. Ruth Trimboli was interested in working on place and notions of belonging, drawing on Aboriginal studies, and having her students participate in various forms of critical thinking and research.

Over a two year period the children engaged in various practices associated with the development of the Grove Gardens. Amongst many others, these included:

- working with architecture students to design where to best place the windows and doors in a room to let in more light
- working in groups to design and make a model illustrating a key design feature of their proposed garden
- pegging out their proposed design on the school grounds
- explaining their design to preschool students and community members
- undertaking a critical analysis of school grounds – plus, minus, interesting and future
- composing poems about belonging spaces
- viewing and analysing how space in public parks was used
- making models of ideal environments for their pets or the pets they wished they had.

The children thus used a range of modes, media and genres for expressing their ideas, whilst encountering new ways of thinking, representing, and solving problems. They were physically engaged in learning to read and peg out spaces in the school grounds. New linguistic and conceptual resources were made available and illustrated with concrete demonstrations. They met and worked with university students and researchers. They went to new places, such as the architecture studio, Parliament House, the Vietnamese garden etc., and were encouraged to think about how they were designed. They worked with varied materials to convey their meanings and imagined designs. The project and its curriculum translations involved the young people bodily, linguistically, relationally, spatially and materially (see Comber, *et al*, in press). These literacies were demanding, dynamic, social and consequential. For reasons of space here only two examples of the kinds of literacies in which the children were engaged are reported here – the consultation books, and using computer assisted design tools.

This page is the front cover of a laminated book made in class, entitled *Developing the area at the front of our school*. Children in Marg Wells' and

Figure 9.1: Student-made cover of the Consultation Book, designed by Kym

Developing the area at the front of our school

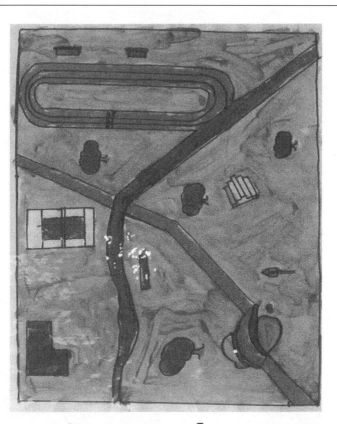

ALEX

What I would like to see in the area?

I would like to see a running track for three, two seats beside the running track, a bird house, some trees, a toilet building, a bridge with a shallow pond, a tennis court, a wall, some platforms and a fence with gates will surround everything I want.

Why?

Because my idea are safe for young children and it will attract people to come here. Also the running track will be great for exercise and some trees will put more oxygen in the air to breathe.

What would it look like? Describe.

The toilet block will be small and red and and inside with be three toilets in boys and girls rooms. The platform will be like stairs that goes very high. The platform will also have rails for safety. The bird house will be small, wooden for birds to go in and out. The bridge will look long and low and the pond will be shallow and clear blue. The court will not take up much space and the tennis court will be light green. The running track will be made out of cement and it will be cream colour. The wall will havbe holes in it for looking through and the wall is red and made out of bricks.

Figure 9.2: A Year Three child's persuasive and visual texts

122

Ruth Trimboli's classes were invited to represent how they would like the garden area to look, using collage, paint, markers, pencil drawings etc. They wrote a text to explain their ideas and persuade readers of their value. The artworks and writing were collated in a book. A blank page was provided next to each design for the children and teachers in other classes to give written feedback. The children wrote persuasive texts of various degrees of complexity to accompany their visual representations. Opposite is one example of Alex, a Year Three child's written and visual text.

The written feedback indicated that other children would have liked more 'interesting things', 'more seats' and 'some shelter'. Some of the young people in the Year Five/Six class wrote extensive texts to make their cases for a garden design and added elaborate visual artworks. 'My garden design' by Kym provides a context for the project and an extended explanation of her design which featured on the front cover as well as in the book.

My Garden Design

Room 1 and room 15 have been involved with the University of South Australia designing elements of gardens, sections of gardens or whole gardens. The design I have created is a bridge. It goes over a shimmering pond and has two paths connecting it.

Our bridge is a long arch over a sparkling pond. There are big trees with statues of native animals everywhere. The bridge has a fence on both sides of it so no one will fall in the pond. The fence has fancy circles along it. Coming out from the sides of the bridge is water running down into the pond. Two paths lead to both sides of the bridge. On both sides of the snake-shaped path is a waterway. Underneath the waterway are lights that are waterproof. There are seats and bins on the bridge, path and the rest of the section. On one side of the pond there are garden beds full of beautiful, majestic flowers and trees with two statues on both sides of the section. On the other side of the bridge are trees and seats and shade over them. On this side are two other statues. In the pond we hope to have fish and water and water reeds in it. There are rocks around the pond to protect it.

Our section of the garden should be incorporated into the Grove Gardens because our students would like a place where it is peaceful and quiet. This place will make people feel royal and special. It will be very interesting and stunning to have this fabulous outstanding and spectacular section to be part of the Grove Gardens.

Our section is a place where students can talk or relax. This is very imaginative and unique place. Here people can watch and learn about nature. The statues will have information on them about the animal that it is. The trees will hopefully have birds living in them. Everyone will have fun and relax in this place. A garden with seating, shade trees and flowers will be the perfect place to relax and have fun.

Kym (age 11)

Several key features of this school literacy task are significant. Children in each of the classes were working on a shared task, yet they were able, as individuals or in pairs, to express their own ideas using both verbal and visual modes. The literacy task itself was part of a bigger meaningful project. Children's designs formed the basis of the university architectural students' designs. The children's designs and persuasive texts were shared within the entire school community and they received feedback from younger and older children, peers, teachers and parents. And there was an added incentive. A garden design would eventually be decided upon, the structures set up and the planting done. Their designing and imagining was an authentic part of actual place-making. Clearly, schoolchildren can become involved in creating new textual forms which simultaneously allow different imaginings about everyday life and positive identity work (Skinner and Holland, 1996). School literacies are not necessarily limited and limiting. Like local literacies in the wider community, what gets done with literacy in schools is contingent on the imaginations, negotiations and practices of its members. Even where official literacy practices include mandated scripted reading lessons, primary school teachers can make space for creative literacies through the potential curriculum space of science, social studies, the arts, information technologies and so on.

The children also enjoyed experimenting with computer assisted design. While they enjoyed using a range of physical materials to represent their garden designs – recycled cardboard, pop-sticks, cereal boxes, twigs and bark from the school yard and the usual array of school art materials – they also appreciated the chance to use the computer to consider different scenarios. A recent architecture graduate introduced the children and teachers to a software programme which allowed the students to manipulate the architecture students' draft design digitally. This enabled the children to try out different positioning of trees and shrubs, to change the heights and shapes of trees and to view their designs from different perspectives. They had a chance to play with digital design, even as they were inducted into traditional model-making, pegging out and other architectural practices.

The opportunities to learn about design in a range of modes and media over an extended period meant that children could connect with the project in different ways. They could imagine and then review their plans at a later stage; they were part of a community of co-designers. Using computer assisted design had different affordances than the other materials. Working across the range of different representational resources enriched what they brought to the computer design. Their embodied pegging out, group model-making and individual art works allowed them to assemble rich meaning-making tools which contributed to their digital experiments. Across the project young people assembled traditional genres, vocabularies and textual practices, new digital literacies and situation-specific local literacies. This productive mix of literacy practices offers more than the re-cycled literacies usually on offer in schools in poor areas. It allows children to acquire literate practices in the wider context of complex meaning-making and goal-oriented activity. As Kress (2000, p138) observes, a 'curriculum for the future' entails educating 'a different kind of social subject' for an era of social and economic instability. The Ridley Grove pupils had opportunities to imagine, design, negotiate and watch elements of their planning come to fruition. They had to deal with the disappointment of some features they had hoped for not being included in the final plan – such as underground tunnels, bridges, bird houses and statues – the delays in completing the work and then an instance of vandalism on their newly hung art-works. As the assistant principal pointed out, this all helped build their resilience, a quality already essential in their everyday lives and upon which their aspirations for the future will be contingent.

Turn-around pedagogies: Learning to teach inclusive literacies
Teachers like Marg Wells and Ruth Trimboli bring years of pedagogical and life experiences to their work plus a sense of room to move that allows them to take risks with the authorised literacy curriculum. But what happens to the generation of teachers just embarking on their careers in neo-conservative, neo-liberal times? What do they make of literacy teaching in socio-economically disadvantaged schools? To find out, we recruited volunteer recent teacher graduates and asked them to invite a late career mentor to co-research the problem of unequal literacy outcomes as it presented in their different workplaces.

The second project, titled: 'Teachers investigate unequal outcomes: Cross-generational perspectives'[iv], is described in Comber and Kamler (2004, 2005) and Kamler and Comber (2005). Ten early career and ten late career teacher-researchers worked with Barbara Comber and Barbara Kamler to investigate the effects of their practices on different children. We wanted to apply the

125

combined resources of two generations of teachers to make a difference to the literacy development of the children they were most worried about. Over the three years of the project, the teachers assessed the literacy curriculum in their classrooms and its impact on the students who were struggling with school literacies; they read about literacy, poverty and communities and considered the potential of positive metaphors for thinking about class and cultural differences; and with support from the teacher and university research networks they determined how to adapt their curriculum and pedagogies to connect with their most alienated 'at risk' students. Here, I discuss the work of one young male teacher and how he came to design and enact what we have since dubbed 'turn-around pedagogies' (Comber and Kamler, 2004).

Rob Fuller had just graduated when he joined the project. As a first year teacher he was assigned to a primary school in a regional town some 300 kilometres from the capital. Locals described it as a tough town: a barren desert, hot in summer, somewhat remote, where poverty was rife. Racial conflicts were intermittently reported in the state press. In his undergraduate study, Fuller showed strong commitment to social justice, demonstrated in his honours research into critical literacy and his interest in Aboriginal studies. In his first year as a teacher he was appointed part-time to a Year Two/Three class and also took up a position as Aboriginal Education Teacher.

Despite Fuller's desire to foreground equity through his literacy curriculum, he found it difficult to engage certain of his pupils in the curriculum and many were struggling with formal school literacy. His co-teacher and mentor worked with him to set up a two-hour 'literacy block' where they rotated groups through different activities and tried to concentrate their teaching efforts explicitly on the children who were having difficulties. They were especially concerned for two Aboriginal boys who resisted participating in the oral or written aspects of set tasks. One of them, Bill, had been assessed as having several language difficulties including dyslexia, speech and articulation difficulties, separation anxiety, a lack of phonemic awareness and poor auditory memory. Bill refused to speak in public and could not read independently.

Fuller had started his teaching career politically committed and idealistic, but he found it hard to get past the official labels for failure to learn that were applied in the school context. Working with his late career mentor Di Hood and the wider network of teacher and university researchers, Fuller reconsidered what he knew about Bill. In the context of the research he read a range of researchers who took a positive stance on what poor and minority children brought to school. Luis Moll and colleagues' (Moll *et al*, 1992) notion of 'funds of knowledge' and Pat Thomson's (2002) 'virtual school-bag' were part of a collection of positive metaphors that the researchers signalled to the teachers in an attempt to change our collective professional vocabularies. This would be the first step in getting out of the pervasive deficit discourses that often prevail in discussions about socio-economic disadvantaged young people (Comber, 1998; Comber and Kamler, 2004).

Influenced by this reading and discussion, Fuller contacted Bill's parents in order to learn more about his out-of-school life and interests. He discovered the family's commitment to freeing refugees from detention, their leisure pre-ferences, such as camping and sports, and the extra support they provided at home to assist Bill with his speech impediment. On a school camp, Fuller observed Bill in different contexts, such as leading his peers in constructing a 'humpy' – an Aboriginal bush shelter built out of sticks and bark. Unlike the shy and reserved child of the classroom, here Bill was directing and negotiat-ing, confident in his knowledge and experience and in teaching his peers (see Fuller and Hood, 2005). Fuller was learning about a different Bill, a child with significant cultural knowledge and expertise. The challenge was how to design a curriculum that allowed Bill to make use of his funds of knowledge and rich resources in acquiring a repertoire of literate practice in the school context. Importantly, Fuller and Hood were seeing what Bill could do in a variety of situations with different participation structures and they learned the value of observing learners in different settings. It allowed them to break out of the normative diagnoses which had positioned Bill as deficient. Armed with this new knowledge, they abandoned their literacy block organisation and re-designed their literacy curriculum in ways that allowed the children to make use of expertise they already had or were developing. To illustrate their altered approach I briefly describe just one curriculum unit, put together soon after the school camp.

Fuller and Hood designed an assignment that responded to the enthusiasm and confidence they had seen in Bill and his peers on camp. The class was to produce a camping magazine, incorporating a range of text types integrated across different curriculum areas. It would carry product reviews, safety tips, campfire stories and procedures for pitching a tent. Not far into this project the children began arguing about the correct sequence for pitching a tent and found it difficult to write the instructions. Fuller decided to take the tent out again and let the children experiment. They were to agree on and record the correct order of pitching, using the school's digital camera. They would then base their procedural text, 'how to pitch a tent', on the photos illustrating the key moves in sequence. When they started writing they began to understand the need for precise language and edited their texts accordingly. Bill was able to use the digital camera as a memory aid and the visual record gave him the prompts which scaffolded his writing. Fuller and Hood reported that 'as a result of these interventions, Bill exhibited a range of behaviours that indicated a positive shift in his use of literacy for making meaning and, more importantly, allowed him to renegotiate his identity within the classroom' (Fuller and Hood 2005, p73).

In terms of our notion of 'turn-around pedagogies', Fuller had turned to the family to learn about Bill. Rather than a one-off conversation, he developed a reciprocal respectful relationship where he learned about Bill from his parents. He had then watched Bill in contexts where he presented differently as a learner and as a peer. Fuller also turned to research to discover more productive ways of understanding Bill as a learner and also to consider literacy as dynamic social practice, rather than as a normative developmental sequence. Thus he was willing to turn around to his students, their parents, his colleagues and the wider educational research community to make sense of his pedagogical challenges and take responsibility for them. He avoided maintaining the cycle of blaming the child and the family.

None of this is easy, especially in the first years of teaching. However, if brave and dedicated young teachers are to teach in challenging schools, the educational community needs to take responsibility for their ongoing learning as teachers. Fuller 'knew' much of the theory of inclusive literacy teaching before he started work. Learning how to make it work *in situ* was not only about assembling practical pedagogical classroom repertoires but also about not being blinded by bureaucratic aspects of teaching, the pervasive negativity of certain older colleagues, and the climate of neo-conservative policy and media rhetoric in which he began his teaching career.

Fuller was one of a two-state network of twenty teachers who joined us on a three-year research project designed to make a difference to the learners whose literacy concerned them. There were children who had been excluded from school because of violent behaviour, children with severe learning and social difficulties, adolescents in poorer communities, both urban and regional, who were alienated from schooling and children from linguistic and cultural heritages other than English. Though the teachers were working in very different schools located in quite different communities, in the project they shared vital approaches to making a serious and positive difference to young people's literacy learning.

Working with the research network, each teacher had first to recognise professional blind-spots, a kind of pedagogical tunnel vision. They needed to find ways of understanding their learners that were not based only on normative judgements and diagnoses of identified student weaknesses. In order to break out of deficit models of thinking they needed to value and exploit the funds of knowledge and cultural resources of their pupils and adopt positively-framed metaphors such as Pat Thomson's virtual school-bag, which proved to be critical. Thomson's argument is that all children arrive at school with full back-packs, but that only some children are able to make use of what is inside. Other children may be excluded from making use of the resources they have. Indeed, these resources may never even appear. For example, Fuller identified the resources Bill had by talking with him and his family and he actively created opportunities for Bill to use what he already knew to help him acquire new repertoires of practices, such as learning to write.

This move was crucial in all cases. The teachers had to move from a 'these-kids-cannot' stance to a 'what-do-I-need-to-do-so-that-these-kids-can' stance. We called this taking pedagogical responsibility for children's learning. This hardly needs saying, but in an over-diagnosing society, it is important that teachers believe they can and should teach *all* their students, even those most disconnected from schooling. Closing the gap depends on teacher belief and action. Yet at various times during the project we witnessed serious self-doubts and sometimes fear in the teachers about being able to foster durable literate identities. Shifting to an investigative orientation was crucial in overcoming this paralysis. When the teachers began to research their students in different learning contexts, they began to make the students' learning the object of study, rather than it remaining a static unsolvable problem. Once teachers opened up to the possibility that a learner might operate differently in different situations, new curriculum options, new pedagogical moves and new contracts for teaching and learning became possible. By shifting to an investigative orientation the teachers could develop a researcher disposition and see their students of concern in new ways. In the research collective the teachers gradually assembled observation and analytic repertoires. They began to notice how students operated in different activities and settings. They identified cognitive and discursive shifts in their students and began to see what was making a difference and how and why these changed practices were taking effect. Closing the gaps requires seeing learners differently, so that teachers can consciously re-imagine and re-make literacy curriculum and pedagogy.

Getting out more

Sometimes the most exciting opportunities for youth growing up in poverty to acquire contemporary representational means for doing significant identity work through literacy occur in out-of-school time and place (Hull and James, in press; Hull and Schultz, 2001; Schultz, 2002). Research on out-of-school literacies demonstrates what disadvantaged youth can do when the conditions are right and shows the implications for pedagogy in schools. Also needed is research that makes visible school pedagogies and school literacies which are making a difference to particular groups of children. So the kinds of in-school pedagogic practices which are positive and productive need to be analysed, especially in schools where children and their families experience high levels of socio-economic disadvantage (see Hayes *et al*, 2006). As researchers have noted, schools have 'overwhelming potential for shaping minds, bodies, and social futures' (Skinner and Holland, 1996, p273). Many researchers have documented the ways in which schools selectively shut down opportunities for poor and working-class youth while other schools are actively working to produce different school and life trajectories.

For over two decades my colleagues and I have sought out counter-stories of teaching literacy in disadvantaged schools (Comber and Nixon, 1999; Comber, Thomson and Wells, 2001; Nixon and Comber, 2005) and we are still working on it[v]. Yet the stories told in this chapter do not do justice to the complexity of teachers' work and its effects. It is still much easier to show how things go wrong for socio-economically disadvantaged schoolchildren, to bemoan how the gaps in literacy achievement are widening, and to despair about new divisions between those with access to new information and communication technologies and those who are excluded. Thus it is all the more necessary to scrutinise the complex work of teachers who succeed against the odds, teachers who make available contemporary literacy practices which have currency and durability.

Our work shows clearly that sustaining such teachers means helping them to get out more – to move outside their classrooms in order to better see what is happening within them. It may mean giving teachers the space and time to visit the classrooms of colleagues, to return to university, to meet parents of their students and to take their classes into the local community and beyond. Breaking out of the intellectual confines of deficit or normativity may require traversals into other institutions as well as theoretical journeys and dialogic inquiries. Young people in these classrooms are assembling literacies they could see made a difference in their worlds. Their literacy practices had social and material consequences. These literacies are likely to be durable to reposition learners as agents with imagination and repertoires of practices which allow them to take action and see themselves in different futures.

Notes

i The project was conducted by Barbara Comber, Helen Nixon and Louise Ashmore from the Centre for Studies in Literacy, Policy and Learning Cultures, Stephen Loo, Louis Laybourne School of Architecture and Design and Jackie Cook, School of Information, Communication and New Media, University of South Australia with teachers, Marg Wells and Ruth Trimboli and young people from Ridley Grove R-7 School, Woodville Gardens, South Australia.

ii We secured funding from a philanthropic foundation in Victoria, Australia, known as the Myer Foundation which supports projects related to social justice and socioeconomic disadvantage, but is not a research funding body. See the Myer Foundation web-site at http://www.myerfoundation.org.au/main.asp. The views expressed in this paper are those of the author only and do not necessarily represent those of the Myer Foundation.

iii Adelaide summer months (when schools are on their long vacation) are notoriously hot and dry. The planting will need to be done when the children and their teachers can organise a watering roster.

iv The *Teachers investigate unequal literacy outcomes: Cross-generational perspectives* research project was funded by the Australian Research Council DP 0208391 (2002-2004) and was granted to Barbara Comber, University of South Australia and Barbara Kamler, Deakin University. The views reported here are those of the author only.

v The projects reported here were conducted with numerous colleagues from the university and school sectors. I wish to acknowledge Helen Nixon, Louise Ashmore, Stephen Loo, Jackie Cook, Marg Wells, Ruth Trimboli, Frank Cairns and Kaye Wieland in the *Urban renewal from the inside-out* project and Barbara Kamler, Lyn Kerkham, Kirsten Hutchison on the *Teachers Investigate Unequal Outcomes: Cross-generational Perspectives* project for their contributions to my learning.

10

UNCOMFORTABLE SPACES

Eve Bearne and Jackie Marsh

M any of the recurring themes of this book are about oppositions: between the 'advantaged' and 'disadvantaged'; between home and school experiences of literacy; between what is seen and recognised and what is hidden and not given value. In the gaps between each of these oppositions lie issues of power. Literacy is deeply related to power – not only because those who 'have literacy' can exercise more power over their lives than those who do not, but also because those who have the power to define what counts as valid and valuable literacy hold the greatest power. Getting hold of literacy can be exclusive as well as inclusive; the ways texts are made, mediated and given value or status are part of wider cultural practices to do with power. The contributions to this book use research, theory and descriptions of pedagogic interventions and practices to think through the tensions and complexities of social and educational inclusion and to offer an agenda for narrowing some of the gaps.

Social exclusion is a process which operates at individual, community and governmental levels. Taking the individual first, another recurrent theme in many of the chapters in the book is about the development of individual identity and identification set within particular cultural and community practices. In just the same way as exclusion operates as a process, so identity is also a process, often of contradictions, being constructed against the grain of dominant practices as well as shaped or affected by them (Gee, 2000; Miedema and Wardekker 1999; Rutherford, 1990). Educational policy and practice can create barriers for identity formation and a major theme in this book is about how pedagogic practices might address some of these oppositions, contradictions and gaps.

At community level, a thread running through many of the chapters is the connection between social and educational exclusion and government policy. Again there is an emphasis on complexity and plurality in thinking about the relationship between communities, families and literacy. Policy can all too easily fall into a deficit view of homes, parents and children, defining them as 'effective' or 'failing' rather than acknowledging the diversity of home literacy experience and the potentials of learners from different backgrounds. In describing a range of projects aimed at supporting groups who might in some definitions be seen as 'at risk' Amanda Hatton and Jackie Marsh and Viv Bird raise some questions about the relationship between government policy and funding and initiatives aimed at closing some of the gaps created by social exclusion. The effects of the 'Read Away Derby' project and the witness of the looked after young people argue strongly for sustained funding if initiatives to support socially excluded groups are to make a difference. In describing and analysing the government's Literacy and Social Inclusion Project, Viv Bird, too, sees sustained funding as 'a policy challenge' (p20) and identifies partnerships and collaborations as essential to breaking the cycle of disadvantage which characterises the position of many socially excluded groups. Debates around policy can often remain at the level of words. The challenge is to turn policy into sustained and collective practice.

Raymond Williams argued that responsible theory which informs change should be 'analytically constructive as well as constructively analytic' (Williams, 1981:233). By this careful distinction he was suggesting that instead of simply analysing the social relations of cultural production a society should use that analysis to take a hand in shaping and reconstructing definitions of cultural production. Critical thinking has to be matched by critical practice. This is just as relevant now as it was when Williams first developed the formulation and it reflects the spirit of this book. As Barbara Comber argues, it is still much easier to identify and 'bemoan how the gaps in literacy achievement are widening ... and despair about new divisions' than to develop pedagogic practices which might tackle the complexities of the social and material consequences of inequity. Interwoven through the different perspectives taken by contributors to this book are issues of policy, pedagogy and identity and, particularly, the challenges and discomforts in trying to promote social and educational equity.

Assumptions and expectations

There are dangers in making assumptions about what learners know or can do, as several contributors point out. Of course, everyday social encounters often involve categorisations and opinions formed without a great deal of foundation. But this is not appropriate in educational settings. For the individuals and groups of learners described in the book such easy, and sometimes damaging, categorisations can have life-changing consequences. Whether these are looked after children assumed to be low attaining; boys described as under-achievers; disaffected learners or young people growing up in poverty, generalisations about what they can or cannot do readily harden into assumed 'facts'. Adverse attitudes can also set up resistant practices so that school or formal literacy settings are seen as at the very least uninspiring and at the worst irrelevant or antagonistic. Current instrumental approaches to literacy, often designed to promote higher achievement, can have the opposite effects from those intended, engendering resistance and opposition in learners (Powell, McIntyre and Rightmyer, 2006). Teaching programmes aimed at 'fixing' perceived problems often exacerbate and deepen social and educational divisions.

One of the themes emerging from the contributions to this book gives some hope in the face of a somewhat depressing landscape of instrumental literacy interventions. The challenge of engaging and sustaining the interest of older disaffected learners, which was met by the Young People Speak Out (YSPO) programme in a variety of ways, offers an insight into the possibilities of transformative practice. Julia Davies and Kate Pahl identify a pedagogy founded on a desire to use the concerns and interests of the young learners themselves as a starting point for offering them the means to take their learning further. This meant not only uncovering their funds of knowledge (Moll *et al*, 1992) but offering ways to 'deepen their understandings and broaden their perspectives on their own and others' lives' (p90). 'Strategic interventions' (Leander and Sheehy, 2004) of this kind also involved 'strategic integration' (Moje *et al*, 2004) of the literacy knowledge that they brought to and experienced in the classroom. Similarly, Barbara Comber's accounts of 'turn-around pedagogies' characterises the kinds of approaches which make a difference – not founded on assumptions and generalisations but representing a 'reciprocal respectful relationship' (p128) between learners and teacher. Both these accounts identify hallmarks of transformative pedagogic practices: openness to other people's perspectives; jointly constructed activities and taking account of student identities as members of particular and differing cultural groups. Comber emphasises the value of 'seeing learners differently' (p129) rather than making limiting assumptions about what learners can – or more damagingly cannot – do.

Shifting assumptions and expectations often means making invisible literacy practices visible. To do so exposes literate, cultural and individual identities. However, identity is neither fixed nor singular but shifting, multiple and ambiguous and recognising the plurality and complexity of students' literate identities places a responsibility on practitioners. Eve Gregory describes young bilingual learners of different social and educational backgrounds who *take hold* of literacy (p52) in ways that often remain invisible to their teachers at school. They construct reading identities from their lived cultural and community experience which – often unnoticed – intersect with schooled practices. Similarly, Mark Vicars' account of a gay man's reading identity deals with invisible and unrecognised interactions and identifications with texts. Both chapters present narratives of literary and cultural experience, offering a reminder that identity is constructed through the stories we tell about – and to – ourselves. They also hint at the silences and gaps in narratives as we select what we tell to whom in different circumstances.

In describing the reading practices of culturally marginalised communities, Gregory and Vicars highlight two important aspects of literate identities and pedagogic practices. The first is that formal educational settings can often close down possibilities for realising identity. This is not to suggest that teachers deliberately ignore what learners bring to the classroom – although sometimes they do – but that in the urge to carry out the responsibility of introducing and sustaining successful schooled literacy, teachers may silence learners. The second point is that in the rush to teach literacy it is easy not to notice that, in Vicars' words, 'many of our students are reading between the lines, beyond the book and off the screen' (p87). Rather than excluding individual and community experience, the literacy curriculum – and the teachers who mediate it – should help 'explore the boundaries and exclusions we have accommodated on the way to constructing our social identities' (Silin, 2003: 262). Like identity, literacy needs to be understood not as a single entity but as a process developed through a series of overlapping experiences and practices.

The digital world and the curriculum

Part of a developing sense of what literacy means and implies is a view of how new forms of text have an impact on the social and educational positioning of learners. There are paradoxes and conflicts in developing policy and constructing the literacy curriculum at a period of significant technological change. Gunther Kress puts it like this:

> Educational policy just has to start from an attempt to understand what the new social situation actually is rather than to continue to attempt to maintain 19th century social relations into the 21st century in all ways. (Kress, 2005, p298)

He argues that the discontinuity between the 'real social situation' and the curriculum is:

> one of the major problems for young people in schools, the gap between the expectations that they bring from their world and the expectations that exist in the school from a former world. (Kress, *ibid*, p294)

A key theme of this book is the tension between school and out-of-school textual experience and the effects on learners of the gap between expectations of texts and their uses and pleasures. As Victoria Carrington urges, it is important to make a rigorous scrutiny of the literacy curriculum and work to revise it so that it genuinely includes digital texts alongside print and not as 'hooks to traditional patterns and outcomes' (p113). To do otherwise is a significantly exclusive act.

Tackling the demands of new forms of texts, the different modes and media in which they appear, and the social practices associated with them is challenging. Opening the classroom to unfamiliar forms of text can seem risky. The strategic interventions described in several chapters of this book present a view of teachers who have been prepared to run with ambiguity, complexity and uncertainty as they strive to develop more inclusive literacy practices. However, the very fact that their work is presented here suggests that there are those who have not embraced the challenges and demands of 21st century social, textual and educational relations. This is not to suggest a deliberately wrong-headed and recalcitrant attitude but more, perhaps, to indicate the pressures and constraints of the politics of literacy and curriculum.

Teachers, like learners, are subject to the political imperatives of a curriculum planned to produce a citizenship which reflects government ideology. State requirements for particular levels of achievement in literacy, inspections and evaluations of educational institutions and teachers, funding arrangements, professional routes to advancement – all these have their impact on how teachers perceive their professional responsibilities. On the one hand they spend their working days with children and young people whose progress they keenly wish to promote; on the other hand they are held accountable to deliver results. These imperatives often work in tension with each other. As Barbara Comber points out, they are often separated from the communities which surround their schools. They are denied the spaces for reflection afforded by visiting other schools, working in partnership with other teachers, enhancing their own professional knowledge.

The effects on teaching are profound, especially now. If teachers are to take on a pedagogy which makes a difference to the learners in their classrooms, then, as Victoria Carrington suggests:

> ...a key pre-requisite for visibility and participation is the ability to 'read' the ways in which we are each positioned in the world by texts and literacy practices and to deploy and manipulate a range of texts and practices to bring about change. (this volume, p104)

If teachers are not familiar with forms of text which children know about, enjoy and use in their communities, both they and their students will be disempowered. Since we live in a multimodal world of representation and communication, having a critical view requires explicit discussion of how texts are constructed through combinations of modes. This can only be done if teachers are aware of the full range of texts and technologies used by young people and alert to ways digital and popular cultural texts are produced. Several chapters in the book explore multimodality as a means of both understanding texts and developing an inclusive pedagogy, but there is significant room for expansion in curriculum, teachers' professional knowledge and everyday practice.

Diversity and difference

Much of this book explores the places and spaces – both metaphorical and actual – in which literacy is experienced and practised. Several chapters explicitly deal with how third space theory can inform analysis of the social and educational tensions and discontinuities between schooled literacy and lived literacy practices. The 'space between' is a gap considered in this book. In his formulation of a hybrid or third space of cultural representation Bhabha (1990) argues that it 'displaces the histories that constitute it, and sets up new structures of authority, new political initiatives' (Bhabha in Rutherford, 1990, p211). This is a challenge to critical thinking and to critical practice. Moje *et al* (2004) use third space theory to identify the sites where students' identities and literate practices are realised, constructed through the creation of hybrid Discourses.

Focusing on the hybridisation of literacy practices allows for the recognition that both out-of-school literacy practices and experiences and in-school practices contribute to shaping student identities. However, there are balances to be kept. As Finders points out:

... it would be morally inept and economically irresponsible if educators in-adequately prepare students from culturally and linguistically diverse back-grounds to meet high academic standards as measured by schools. At the same time, it would be fundamentally irresponsible to neglect students' cul-tural, emotional and social literacies, literacies that are shaped in school and beyond the classroom walls. A hybridisation of literacy practices seeks to find the balance. (Finders, 2005, p390)

On the other hand, Leander and Sheehy (2004) describe the difficulties of steering to a new space between the 'thick and thin spaces' of reproductive practices which dissociate students from lived social experience. The gaps and intersections described by the contributors see space theory as offering a way forward for researching, rethinking and transforming pedagogy.

Some of the spaces are uncomfortable places to be – for learners and for teachers. Bhabha argues that difference offers a space which recognises the productive friction of 'a politics based on unequal, uneven, multiple and *potentially antagonistic* political identities (p208)' (italics in original). This is an unsettling way of looking at the construction of cultural identities, rights and responsibilities. However, in the spirit of making the invisible visible, it is a bracing reminder of the jagged edginess of literacy politics. For Bhabha, a view of cultural diversity signals an unacceptable liberal relativist position. Sixteen years on from his original formulation of third space we would argue that the territory has shifted so that diversity is seen rather more positively as an opportunity to recognise the overlapping Discourses which meet in educational spaces. For the contributors to this book diversity and difference are both essential aspects of an inclusive pedagogy. But we hope our stance is not complacent. In drawing together the common themes of the book, we acknowledge that there are gaps and exclusions here, too. Certain mar-ginalised groups are absent, for example particular racial and ethnic com-munities, Travellers, refugees and asylum seekers, young people in offenders' institutions. These omissions indicate just how important it is to continue probing the inequities of social exclusion and advocating pedagogic practices which recognise difference.

This book offers examples of how collaborative endeavours can honour dif-ference whilst also accommodating diversity. They have focused on carefully attentive pedagogic practices and policies designed to close some of the gaps in literacy experience and achievement. The strategic interventions des-cribed here – both within educational settings and outside them – acknow-ledge that literacy and ideology go hand in hand. The stories of those who inhabit particular literacy spaces are witness to the importance of practices which will expand rather than constrain the development of different literate and social identities. The contributors recognise the realities of life in the 21st century and offer insights into ways in which literacy teaching can be energised so that *all* learners can become engaged and assured users and producers of all kinds of multimodal texts. They do not offer easy or comfortable solutions. They describe the insecurities of entering unfamiliar spaces and crossing borders. But the message is constructively analytic, mapping out ways of rethinking and reconfiguring the relationships between literacy, identity, community, policy and pedagogy. Although developing a transformative pedagogy may be edgy and difficult, strategic integration of the range of experiences and funds of knowledge brought to the classroom is essential to redressing social and educational exclusion.

The agenda presented in this book involves: re-examining assumptions and definitions of learners and their literate identities; recognising the friction of difference as a necessary component in reshaping educational policy and practice; accommodating diversity; developing partnerships for collaborative and co-operative practices; and re-examining the texts and practices that make up the literacy curriculum. For governments, this means a commitment to sustained funding and support. For educational institutions and teachers, it means going beyond the walls of the classroom in order to transform practice. For individuals it means the chance to realise literate identities. This agenda will be enacted in a range of spaces – in minds and in meeting places. It may be based on uneven and possibly antagonistic positions but it will seek, through productive friction, to make a difference.

References

Adams, C. (1987) *Across Seven Seas and Thirteen Rivers.* London: THAP Books

Agamben, G. Trans Liz Heron (1993) *Infancy and History: The Destruction of Experience.* London: Verso

Althusser, L. (1968, trans 1970) *Reading Capital.* London. New Left Books

Alvermann, D. (2006) Ned and Kevin: An Online Discussion that Challenges the 'Not-Yet Adult' Cultural Model, in Pahl, K. and Rowsell, J. (2006) (eds) *Travel Notes from the New Literacy Studies: Instances of Practice.* Clevedon: Multilingual Matters

Alverman, D, Moon, J.S. and Hagood, M. C. (1999) *Popular Culture in the Classroom: Teaching and Researching Critical Media Literacy.* Delaware and Illinois: International Reading Association and National Reading Conference

Amit-Talai, V. and Wuff, H. (eds) (1995) *Youth Cultures: A Cross-cultural Perspective.* New York: Routledge

Anderson, B. (1991) *Imagined Communities: Reflections on the Origin and Spread of Nationalism.* London: Verso

Appadurai, A. (1996) *Modernity at Large: Cultural Dimensions of Globalisation.* London: University of Minnesota Press

Apple, M. (2005) Doing things the 'right' way: legitimating educational inequalities in conservative times. *Educational Review* 57 (3) pp 271-193

Appleyard J.A. (1990) *The Experience of Fiction from Childhood to Adulthood.* Cambridge: Cambridge University Press

Arizpe, E. (2001) Responding to a 'Conquistadora': Readers talk about gender in Mexican secondary schools. *Gender and Education* 13 (1) pp 25-37

Asghar, M.A. (1996) *Bangladeshi Community Associations in East London.* London: Bangla Heritage Ltd

Audit Commission (1994) *Seen but not Heard.* London: HMSO

Bakhtin, M. (1984) (trans Helene Iswolsky) *Rabelais and His World.* Bloomington: Indiana University Press

Bald. J. (1982) Children in care need books. *Concern,* 44 pp18-21

Barrs, M. and Cork, V. (2001) *The Reader in the Writer.* London: Centre for Language in Primary Education

Barrs, M. and Pidgeon, S. (eds) (1993) *Reading the Difference: Gender and Reading in the Primary School.* London: Centre for Language in Primary Education

Barrs, M. and Pidgeon, S. (eds) (2002) *Boys and Writing.* London: Centre for Literacy in Primary Education

Barton, D. (1994) *Literacy: An Introduction to the Ecology of Written Language*. Oxford: Blackwell

Bearne, E. (2003) Playing with Possibilities: Children's multidimensional texts, in Bearne, E., Dombey, H. and Grainger, T. (eds) *Classroom Interactions in Literacy*. Buckingham: Open University Press

Bernstein, B. (1973) Social class, language and socialisation, in Abramson, A.S. *et al.* (eds) *Current Trends in Linguistics*, 12. Amsterdam: Mouton Press

Bhabha, H.K. (1990) The Third Space, in Rutherford, J. (ed) *Identity, Community Culture, Difference*. London: Lawrence and Wishart

Bhabha, H.K. (1994) *The Location of Culture*. London: Routledge

Bigum, C. (2004) Rethinking Schools and Community: The knowledge producing school, in Marshall, S., Taylor, W. and Yu, X. (eds) *Using Community Informatics to Transform Regions*. Pennsylvania: Idea Group Inc.

Bird, V. (2004) *Literacy and Social Inclusion: The Policy Challenge. A Discussion Paper.* National Literacy Trust. The discussion paper was launched at a seminar at 11 Downing Street. The paper and the full report of the event and debate can be downloaded from www.smith-institute.org.uk

Bird, V. (2005) The Literacy and Social Inclusion Project: A new model for building parental skills. *Literacy*, 39 (2) pp 59-63

Bird, V. and Akerman, R. (2005) *Every Which Way We Can. London: National Literacy Trust.* See www.literacytrust.org.uk/socialinclusion

Bird, V. and Akerman, R. (2005) *Literacy and Social Inclusion: The Handbook*. London: National Literacy Trust

Blackburn, M.V. (2002) Disrupting the (hetero)normative: Exploring literacy performances and identity work with queer youth. *Journal of Adolescent and Adult Literacy* 46 (2) pp 312-324

Blackburn, M. V. (2003) Exploring literacy performances and power dynamics at The Loft: Queer youth reading the world and the word. *Research in the Teaching of English* 37 (4) pp 467-490

Blommaert, J., Collins, J. and Slembrouck, S. (2004) *Spaces of Multilingualism. Working Papers on Language, Power and Identity No 18*. Accessed December, 2005 at: http://bank. rug.ac.be/lpi/LPI18.pdf

Booth, D. and Neelands, J. (eds) (1998) *Writing in Role: Classroom Projects Connecting Writing and Drama*. Hamilton, Ontario: Caliburn Enterprises

Bowman, S. and Willis, C. (2003) *We Media: How Audiences are Shaping the Future of News and Information*. Commissioned by the Media Center at The American Press Institute. Accessed February, 2006 at: www.hypergene.net/wemedia/

Bourdieu, P. (1986) The Forms of Capital, in Richardson, J.G. *Handbook for Theory and Research for the Sociology of Education* pp 241-258 Westport CT: Greenwood Press

Brandt, D. and Clinton, K. (2002) Limits of the local: expanding perspectives on literacy as a social practice. *Journal of Literacy Research* 34(3) pp 337-356

British Broadcasting Corporation (BBC) (2005) *How mobiles changed the face of news.* Review 2005. Broadcast available. Accessed February, 2006 at: http://news.bbc.co.uk/nolavconsole/ukfs_news/hi/newsid_4550000/ newsid_4553800/bb_rm_4553802.stm

British Toy and Hobby Association (2006) *The year in toys 2005*. Accessed February, 2006at: http://www.btha.co.uk/press/year_in_toys.php

Britzman, D.P. (1997). What is this thing called love? New discourses for understanding gay and lesbian youth, in de Castell, S. and Bryson, M. (eds) *Radical Interventions: Identity, Politics, and Difference/s on Educational Praxis.* Albany: State University of NewYork Press

Brooks, G., Gorman, T., Harman, J., Hutchison, D. and Wilkin, A. (1996) *Family Literacy Works: The NFER Evaluation of the Basic Skills Agency's Demonstration Programmes.* London: Basic Skills Agency

Bullock Report (1975) *A Language for Life: Report of the Committee of Inquiry Appointed by the Secretary of State for Education and Science.* London: HMSO

Bynner, J. (2003) *Risks and Outcomes of Social Exclusion: Insights from Longitudinal Data.* London: Institute of Education

Byrne, D. (1999) *Social Exclusion.* Buckingham: Open University Press

Byrne, D. (2005) *Social Exclusion.* (2nd edn). Buckingham: Open University Press

Carlyle, T. (1831) *Sartor Resartus: The Life and Opinions of Herr Teufelsdrockh.* Accessed at: http://cupid.ecom.unimelb.edu.an/het/carlyle/sartor.html. on November 5th 2006

Castells, M. (2000) *The Rise of the Network Society.* Oxford: Blackwell

Centre for Economic and Social Inclusion (2002) *Social Inclusion.* Accessed April, 2006 at: http://www.cesi.org.uk/kbdocs/socinc.doc

de Certeau, M. (trans. Steven Rendell) (1984) *The Practice of Everyday Life.* London: University of California Press

Cieslik, M. and Simpson, D. (2005) *The Role of Basic Skills in Transitions to Adulthood.* Middlesbrough: School of Social Sciences and Law, University of Teesside

Clark, C. and Foster, A. (2005) *Children's and Young People's Reading Habits and Preferences: The Who, What, Why, Where and When.* London: National Literacy Trust

Clark, C. and Rumbold, K. (2006) *Reading for Pleasure: A Research Overview.* London: National Literacy Trust

Cochran-Smith, M. (1984) *The Making of a Reader.* Norwood, NJ: Ablex

Coffield , D., Mosely, D., Hall, K. and Ecclestone, E. (2004) *A Systematic and Critical Review of Learning Styles and Pedagogy.* London: Learning and Skills Development Agency

Coles, G. (1999) *Literacy, Emotions, and the Brain: An Invited Contribution.* Reading Online. Accessed April, 2006 at: http://www.readingonline.org/critical/coles.html

Comber, B. (1998) Problematising 'Background': (Re)constructing categories in educational research. *Australian Educational Researcher* 25 (3) pp1-21

Comber, B. (2001) Critical literacies and local action: teacher knowledge and a 'new' research agenda. In Comber, B. and Simpson, A. (eds) *Negotiating Critical Literacies in classrooms.* New Jersey: Lawrence Erlbaum

Comber, B. and Kamler, B. (eds) (2005) *Turn-around Pedagogies: Literacy Interventions for At-risk Students.* Newtown, NSW: Primary English Teaching Association

Comber, B. and Kamler, B. (2004) Getting out of deficit: Pedagogies of reconnection. *Teaching Education* 15(3) pp293-310

Comber, B and Nichols, S. (2004) Getting the big picture: regulating knowledge in the early childhood literacy curriculum. *Journal of Early Childhood Literacy* 4 (1) pp43-63

Comber, B. and Nixon, H. (1999) Literacy education as a site for social justice: what do our practices do? in Edelsky, C. (ed) *Making Justice our Project: Critical Whole Language Teachers Talk About Their Work.* Urbana, Illinois: National Council of Teachers of English

Comber, B. and Nixon, H. (2005) Children Re-Read and Re-Write their Neighbourhoods: Critical literacies and identity work, in Evans, J. (ed) *Literacy Moves On: Using Popular Cul-*

ture, *New Technologies and Critical Literacy in the Primary Classroom*. Portsmouth: Heinemann

Comber, B., Nixon, H., Ashmore, L., Loo, S. and Cook, J. (in press) Urban Renewal from the Inside Out: Spatial and critical literacies in a low socioeconomic school community. *Mind, Culture and Activity* 12(3)

Comber, B., Thomson, P. and Wells, M. (2001) Critical literacy finds a 'place': Writing and social action in a neighbourhood school. *Elementary School Journal* 101(4) pp 451-464.

Connell, J. (2000) Aesthetic Experiences in the School Curriculum: Assessing the value of Rosenblatt's transactional theory. *Journal of Aesthetic Education* 34 pp 1-9

Connell, R. W. (1989) Cool guys, swots and wimps: The interplay of masculinity and education. *Oxford Review of Education* 15 pp 291-303

Connell, R. W. (1995) *Masculinities*. Cambridge: Polity Press

Connell, R. W. (2000) *The Men and the Boys*. Cambridge: Polity Press

Connolly, P. (2006) The Effects of Social Class and Ethnicity on Gender Differences in GCSE Attainment: a secondary analysis of the youth cohort study of England and Wales 1998. *British Educational Research Journal* 32 (1) pp3-21

Cope, B. and Kalantzis, M. (eds) (2000) *Multiliteracies: Literacy Learning and the Design of Social Futures*. London: Routledge

Crumpler, T. and Tchneider, J. (2002) Writing with Their Whole Being: a cross study analysis of children's writing from five classrooms using process drama. *Research in Drama Education* 7 (2) pp 61-79

Davies, J. (2005) *Evaluation of the Sheffield College/Sheffield LEA Literacy through Technology Project*. Accessed February, 2006 at: http://my.sheffcol.ac.uk/index.cfm?ParentID=B3E77A69-64EA-4B91-87E7-ED55BC42FCE

Davies, J. (2006) Escaping to the Borderlands: an exploration of the Internet as a cultural space for teenaged Wiccan girls, in: Pahl, K. and Rowsell, J. (eds) *Travel Notes from the New Literacy Studies: Instances of Practice*. Clevedon: Multilingual Matters

Davies, J. (2006b) Nomads and tribes: online meaning making and the development of new literacies, in Marsh, J. and Millard, E. (eds) *Popular Literacies, Childhood and Schooling*. London: Routledge

Davies, W. (2005) Don't assume that improving IT alone will breach the digital divide. *The Times*, 25th January 2005. Accessed December, 2005 at: http://www.ippr.org/articles/index.asp?id=508

Department for Education and Employment (DfEE) (1998) *National Literacy Strategy*, London: Her Majesty's Stationery Office

Department for Education and Employment (1999) *Circular 10/99 Social Inclusion: Pupil Support*. London: Her Majesty's Stationery Office

Department for Education and Employment/Department of Health (DoH) (1999) *Draft Guidance on the Education of Children Looked After by Local Authorities*. London: Her Majesty's Stationery Office

Department for Education and Skills (1998) *The National Literacy Strategy Framework*. London: HMSO

Department for Education and Skills (DfES) (2000) *Sex and relationships education guidance*. London: Her Majesty's Stationery Office

Department for Education and Skills (2001) *Skills for Life: The national strategy for improving literacy and numeracy skills*. London: Her Majesty's Stationery Office

Department for Education and Skills (2003) *The Skills for Life Survey. A national needs and impact survey of literacy, numeracy and ICT skills.* DfES Research Brief RB 490. London: Her Majesty's Stationery Office

Department for Education and Skills (2004) *Every Child Matters: Next Steps.* London: Her Majesty's Stationery Office

Department for Education and Skills (2005) *Children looked after in England (including adoption and care leavers) 2004-2005.* Statistical First Release. Accessed April, 2006 at: http://www.dfes.gov.uk/rsgateway/DB/SFR/s000615/index.shtml

Department of Education and Science (DES) (1967) *Children and their Primary Schools. (The Plowden Report)* London: Her Majesty's Stationery Office

Department of Education and Science (1975) *A Language for Life. (The Bullock Report)* London: Her Majesty's Stationery Office

Department of Education and Science (1988) *English for Ages 5-11 Proposals of the Secretary of State. (The Cox Report)* London: Her Majesty's Stationery Office

Department of Education and Science (1996) *Desirable Outcomes.* London: Her Majesty's Stationery Office

Department of Health (DoH) (1998) *Quality Protects: Framework for Action.* London: Her Majesty's Stationery Office

Department of Health (2002) *Children's Homes: National Minimum Standards.* London: Her Majesty's Stationery Office

Derrida, J. (1976) *Of Grammatology.* Baltimore: John Hopkins University Press

Desforges, C. and Abouchaar, A. (2003) *The Impact of Parental Involvement, Parental Support and Family Education on Pupil Achievement and Adjustment: A Review of the Literature.* London: Her Majesty's Stationery Office

Dunkel, C.S., and Anthis, K.S. (2001) The role of possible selves in identity formation: a short term longitudinal study. *Journal of Adolescence,* 24 (6) pp765-776

Dyson, A. H. (1997) *Writing Superheroes: Contemporary Childhood, Popular Culture and Classroom Literacy.* New York: Teachers College Press

Dyson, A.H. (2003) *The Brothers and Sisters Learn to Write: Popular Literacies in Childhood and School Cultures.* New York: Teachers College Press

Dyson, A.H. (2006) Foreword: why popular literacies matter, in Marsh, J. and Millard, E. (2006) (eds) *Popular Literacies, Childhood and Schooling.* London: Routledge.

Ellis,V. and High, S. (2004) Something more to tell you: gay, lesbian or bisexual young people's experience of secondary schooling. *British Educational Research Journal,* 30 (2) 213-225

Epstein, D., Elwood, J., Hey, V. and Maw, J. (1998) *Failing Boys? Issues in Gender and Achievement.* Buckingham: Open University Press

Escoffer, J. (1993) Generations and paradigms: Mainstreams in Lesbian and Gay studies. *Journal of Homosexuality* 24 pp 7-26

Essex Writing Project (2002) *More than Mulan: Using Video to Improve Boys' Writing.* Chelmsford: The English Team, Essex Advisory and Inspection Service

Essex Writing Project (2003) *Visually Speaking: Using Multimedia Texts to Improve Boys' Writing.* Chelmsford: The English Team, Essex Advisory and Inspection Service

Euesden, P. and McCullough, K. (2006) Reaching and engaging new learners using popular culture through a blend of online and classroom learning, in Hamilton, M. and Wilson, A. (eds) *New Ways of Engaging New Learners: Lessons from Round One of the Practitioner-led*

Research Initiative. London: National Research and Development Centre for Adult Literacy and Numeracy

Evangelou, M. and Sylva, K. (2003) *The Effects of the Peers Early Education Partnership (PEEP) on Children's Developmental Progress.* London: Department for Education and Skills

Festinger, L. (1957) *A Theory of Cognitive Dissonance.* Evanston, IL: Row, Peterson

Fetterley, J. (1978) *The Resisting Reader: a Feminist Approach to American Fiction.* Bloomington: Indiana University Press

Finders, M. (2005) Hybridization of literacy practices: A review of 'What they don't learn in school: Literacy in the lives of urban youth'. *Reading Research Quarterly* 40 (3) pp 388-397

Fine, M. (1994) Working the Hyphens: Reinventing Self and Other in Qualitative Research, in Denzin, N. and Lincoln, Y. (eds) *Handbook of Qualitative Research* (1st edn). London: Sage

Fisher, D. (2003) Immigrant Closets: Tactical-Micro-Practices-in-the-Hyphen. *Journal of Homosexuality* 45 pp 171-192

Fletcher-Campbell, F. and Hall, C. (1990) *Changing Schools? Changing People? The Education of Children in Care.* Slough: National Foundation for Educational Research.

Flouri, E. and Buchanan, A. (2001) *Father Involvement and Outcomes in Adolescence and Adulthood.* Oxford: Department of Social Policy and Social Work, University of Oxford

Fone, B.R. (1983) This Other Eden: Arcadia and the Homosexual Imagination. *Journal of Homosexuality* 8 pp13-34

Francis, B. (1998) *Power Plays: Primary school children's constructions of gender, power and adult work.* Stoke on Trent: Trentham Books

Francis, B (2000) *Boys, Girls and Achievement: Addressing the Classroom Issues.* London: Routledge/Falmer

Francis, J. (2000) Investing in Children's Futures: Enhancing the educational arrangements of `looked after' children and young people. *Child and Family Social Work* 5: 23-33

Freire, P. (trans M. Ramos) (1972) *Pedagogy of the Oppressed.* Harmondsworth: Penguin

Freire, P. and Macedo, D. (1987) *Literacy: Reading the Word and the World.* London: Bergin and Garvey

Fuller, R. and Hood, D. (2005) Utilising community funds of knowledge as resources for school literacy learning, in Comber, B. and Kamler, B. (eds) *Turn-around Pedagogies: Literacy Interventions for At-risk Students.* Newtown, NSW: Primary English Teaching Association.

Gee, J. P. (1990) *Social Linguistics and Literacies: Ideology in Discourse.* New York: Falmer Press

Gee, J. P. (2000) The New Literacy Studies: From 'socially situated' to the work of the social, in Barton, D., Hamilton, M. and Ivanic, R. (eds) *Situated Literacies: Reading and Writing in Context.* London: Routledge

Gee, J.P. (2004) *Situated Language and Learning: A critique of Traditional Schooling.* London: Routledge

Gere, C. (2002) *Digital Culture.* London: Reaktion Books

Gilbert, P. and Gilbert, R. (2001) Masculinity, inequality and post-school opportunities: disrupting oppositional policies about boys' education. *International Journal of Inclusive Education* 5 pp 1-13

Gillborn, D. (2005) 'It's not a conspiracy ... it's worse than that': a critical race perspective on education after the Stephen Lawrence inquiry. Paper presented at the British Educational Research Association (BERA) Annual Conference, University of Glamorgan, 2005

Gillborn, D. and Mirza, H.S. (2000) *Educational Inequality: Mapping Race, Class and Gender.* London: Her Majesty's Stationery Office

Goddard.J. (2000) The Education of Looked After Children. *Child and Family Social Work* 5 pp79-86

Gold, K. (1995) Hard times for Britain's lost boys. *New Scientist,* 4th February, pp12-13

Golden, S., Spielhofer, T., Sims, D. and O'Donnell, L. (2004) *Supporting the Hardest-to-Reach Young People: The contribution of the Neighbourhood Support Fund.* London: Department for Education and Skills

Gonzalez, N., Moll, L., and Amanti, C. (eds) (2005) *Funds of Knowledge; Theorizing Practices in Households and Classrooms.* New Jersey: Lawrence Erlbaum Associates

Gorard, S. (2000) One of us cannot be wrong: the paradox of achievement gaps. *British Journal of Sociology* 21 (3) pp391-400

Gorard, S., Rees, G., Salisbury, J. (2001) Investigating the patterns of differential attainment of boys and girls at school. *British Educational Research Journal* 27 (2) pp125-139

Gordon, D., Adelman. L., Ashworth, K., Bradshaw, J., Levitas, R., Middleton, S., Pantazis, C., Patsios, D., Payne, S., Townsend, P., and Williams, J. (2000) *Poverty and Social Exclusion in Britain.* York: Joseph Rowntree Foundation.

Graham, L. (2001) From Tyrannosaurus Rex to Pokemon: autonomy in the teaching of writing. *Reading literacy and language* 35 (3) pp18-26

Grainger, T. Goouch, K. and Lambirth, A. (2005) *Creativity and Writing: Developing Voice and Verve in the Classroom.* London: RoutledgeFalmer

Green, B. (1998) Thinking about students who do not identify as gay, lesbian or bisexual but.... *Journal of American College Health* 47 (2) pp 89-91

Gregory, E. (1996) *Making Sense of a New World: Learning to Read in a Second Language.* London: Sage

Gregory, E. (2005) Guiding Lights: Siblings as Literacy Teachers in a Multilingual Community, in Anderson, J., Kendrick, M., Rogers, T. and Smythe, S. (eds) *Portraits of Literacy across Families, Communities and Schools: Intersections and Tensions.* New Jersey: Lawrence Erlbaum Associates

Gregory, E. and Williams, A. (2000) *City Literacies: Learning to Read across Generations and Cultures.* London: Routledge

Gregory, E., Long, S. and Volk, D. (2004) *Many Pathways to Literacy: Young children Learning with Siblings, Grandparents and Communities.* London and New York: RoutledgeFalmer

Gurian, M. (2001) *Boys and Girls Learn Differently! A Guide for Teachers and Parents.* San Francisco, CA: Jossey-Bass

Hagood, M.C. (2004) A Rhizomatic Cartography of Adolescents' Popular Culture, and Constructions of Self, in Leander, K. and Sheehy, M. (eds) *Spatialising Literacy Research and Practice.* New York: Peter Lang

Hall.C. and Coles. M. (1999) *Children's Reading Choices.* London: Routledge

Hamilton, M. and Wilson, A. (eds) (2006) *New Ways of Engaging New Learners: Lessons from Round One of the Practitioner-led Research Initiative.* London: National Research and Development Centre for Adult Literacy and Numeracy

Hannon, P., Pahl, K., Bird, V., Taylor, C. and Birch, C. (2003) *Community-Focused Provision in Adult Literacy, Numeracy and Language: An Exploratory Study.* London: National Research and Development Centre for Adult Literacy and Numeracy

Harker. R.M., Dobel-Ober. D, Lawrence. J., Berridge, D. and Sinclair, R. (2003) Who Takes Care of Education? Looked after children's perceptions of support for educational progress. *Child and Family Social Work* 8 pp 89-100

Hatton, A. (2005) The Reality of Reading: A study into the attitudes, practices and experiences of young people in residential care. Unpublished MA Dissertation. Sheffield: University of Sheffield

Hayes, D., Mills, M., Christie, P., and Lingard, B. (2006) *Teachers and Schooling Making a Difference: Productive Pedagogies, Assessment and Performance.* Sydney: Allen and Unwin

Heath, S.B. (1983) *Ways with Words: Language, Life and Work Across Communities and Classrooms.* Cambridge: Cambridge University Press

Her Majesty's Treasury (2005) *Support for Parents: The Best Start for Children.* London. Her Majesty's Stationery Office

Hermida, A. (2002) *Mobile money spinner for women.* BBC Online News. Accessed February, 2006 at: http://news.bbc.co.uk/1/techology/2254231.stm

Herr, K. (1997) Learning Lessons from School: Homophobia, heterosexism and the construction of failure, in Harris, M. (ed) *School Experiences of Gay and Lesbian Youth: The Invisible Minority.* London: Harrington Park Press

Hewison, J. and Tizard, J. (1980) Parental Involvement and Reading Attainment. *British Journal of Educational Psychology* 50 pp 209-15

Higgins, C. (2002) Using Film to Support Reluctant Writers. *English in Education,* 36 (1) pp 25-37

Hills, J. and Stewart, K. (eds) (2004) *New Labour, Poverty, Inequality and Exclusion,* Bristol: Policy Press

Holland, D., Lachicotte, W., Skinner, D. and Cain, C. (2001) *Identity and Agency in Cultural Worlds.* Harvard: Harvard University Press

Hull, G. and James, M. A. (in press) Geographies of hope: A study of urban landscapes and a university-community collaborative, in O'Neill, P. (ed) *Blurring Boundaries: Developing Writers, Researchers, and Teachers.* Cresskill, NJ: Hampton Press

Hull, G., and Schultz, K. (2001) Literacy and learning out of school: A review of theory and research. *Review of Educational Research* 71 (4) pp 575-611

Hull, G. and Schultz, K. (eds) (2002) *School's Out: Bridging Out-of-school Literacies with Classroom Practice.* New York: Teachers College Press

Ingraham, C. (1997) The Heterosexual Imaginary: Feminist sociology and theories of gender, in Hennessy, R. and Ingraham, C. (eds) *Materialist Feminism: A Reader in Class Difference and Women's Lives.* New York: Routledge

Ito, M. (2005) Technologies of the Childhood Imagination: Yugioh, media mixes, and everyday cultural production, in Karaganis, J. and Jeremijenko, N. (eds) *Structures of Participation in Digital Culture.* New York: Duke University Press

Ito, M., Okabe, D. and Matsuda, M. (eds) (2005) *Personal, Portable, Pedestrian: Mobile phones in Japanese life.* Cambridge: MIT Press

Jackson. S. (1994) Educating children in Residential and Foster Care. *Oxford Review of Education* 20 (3) pp 267-279

Jackson. S (1988-9) Residential Care and Education in *Children and Society* (1988-9), 4, pp.335-350

Jackson, S. and Martin, P. Y. (1998) Surviving the Care System. *Journal of Adolescence* 21 pp 569-583

Jenkins, H. (1992) *Textual Poachers: Television Fans and Participatory Culture.* New York: Routledge

Jessel, J., and Gregory, E., Islam, T., Kenner, C. and Ruby, M. (2004) Children and their grandparents at home: A mutually supportive context for learning and linguistic development. *Journal of English in Education,* 36, 4, pp16-24

Kamberelis, G. (2004) The Rhizome and the Pack: Liminal literacy formations with political teeth, in Leander, K. and Sheehy, M. (eds) *Spatialising Literacy Research and Practice.* New York: Peter Lang

Kamler, B. and Comber, B. (2005) Turn around pedagogies: Improving the education of at risk students. *Improving schools* 8 (2) pp 121-131

Kennard, J. E. (1986) Ourself behind Ourself: A theory for lesbian readers, in Flynn, E. A. and Schweickard, P.P. (eds) *Gender and reading: Essays on Readers, Texts and Contexts.* Baltimore: John Hopkins University Press

Kenner, C. and Gregory, E. (2006-2007) *Bilingual Learning Strategies in School and Community Contexts.* ESRC project

Kerby, A. (1991) *Narrative and the Self.* Bloomington, Indiana University Press

Kotsopoulos, A. (2006) *Reading Against the Grain Revisited.* Accessed January, 2006 at: http://www.ejumpcut.org/archive/jc44.2001/aspasia/againstgrain1.html

Kress, G. (1997) *Before Writing: Rethinking the Paths to Literacy.* London: Routledge

Kress, G. (2003) *Literacy in the New Media Age.* London: Routledge

Kress, G. (2005) Interview with Gunther Kress, in *Discourse: Studies in the Cultural Politics of Education.* 26 (3) pp 287-300

Larson, J. and Marsh, J. (2005) *Making Literacy Real.* London: Paul Chapman

Leander, K. and Sheehy, M. (eds) (2004) *Spatializing Literacy Research and Practice.* New York: Peter Lang

Levin, D. E. and Rosenquest, B. (2001) The Increasing Role of Electronic Toys in the Lives of Infants and Toddlers: Should we be concerned? *Contemporary Issues in Early Childhood* 2(2) pp242-247

Levitas, R. (2005) *The Inclusive Society.* (2nd edition) Basingstoke: Palgrave

Lipman, P. (2005) Metropolitan regions – new geographies of inequality in education: the Chicago metroregion case. *Globalisation, Societies and Education* 3(2) pp141-163

Livingstone, S. and Bober, M. (2004) *UK Children Go Online: Surveying the Experiences of Young People and Their Parents.* London: London School of Economics

Lloyd, S. (2004) *The Jolly Phonics Wordbooks.* Essex: Jolly Learning Ltd

London Borough of Tower Hamlets (1994) *Education Statistics, 1994.* London Borough of Tower Hamlets: Policy and Performance Monitoring Unit

Luke, A. (1998) Getting over method: Literacy teaching as work in new times. *Language Arts* 75 pp 305-313

Luke, A. (2004) Teaching after the marketplace: From commodity to cosmopolitanism. *Teachers College Record* 106 (7) pp1422-1443

Mac an Ghail, M. (1994) *The Making of Men: Masculinities, Sexualities and Schooling.* Buckingham: Open University Press

Mandanipour, A., Cars, G. and Allen, J. (eds) (1998) *Social Exclusion in European Cities.* London: Jessica Kingsley

Markus, H. and Nurius, P. (1986) Possible Selves. *American Psychologist* 41 pp 954- 969

Marsh, J. (2002) Electronic toys: Why should we be concerned? A response to Levin and Rosenquest. *Contemporary Issues in Early Childhood* 3 (1) pp132-137

Marsh, J. (2003) Superhero stories: literacy, gender and popular culture, in Skelton, C. and Francis, B. (eds) *Boys and Girls in the Primary Classroom*. Buckingham: Open University Press

Marsh, J. (2004) *The US! Project: Moving the Bigger Picture On. Final Evaluation Report for the Paul Hamlyn Foundation*. Sheffield: University of Sheffield. Accessed April, 2006 at: http://www.rowa.org.uk/pdfs/125.pdf

Marsh, J. (2006) *New Literacies, Old Identities: Girls' Experiences of Literacy and New Technologies at Home and School*. Paper presented at ESRC-funded Seminar Series: Girls and Education 3-16: Old Concerns, New Agendas. Goldsmiths College, March, 2006

Marsh.J. and Millard. E. (2000) *Literacy and Popular Culture: Using Children's Culture in the Classroom*. London: Paul Chapman/ Sage

Marsh, J. and Millard, E. (eds) (2005) *Popular Literacies, Childhood and Schooling*. London: RoutledgeFalmer

Marsh, J., Hatton, A. and Kings, T. (2006) *Final Evaluation Report of the Read Away Derby Project*. Sheffield: University of Sheffield. (Full evaluation available at www.rowa.org.uk/)

Martin, B. (1996) *Femininity Played Straight: The Significance of Being Lesbian*. New York: Routledge

Martin, D.A. and Hetrick, E.S. (1988) The Stigmatisation of the Gay and Lesbian Adolescent. *Journal of Homosexuality* 16 pp163-83.

Martin, P. Y. and Jackson, S. (2002) Educational success for children in public care: advice from a group of high achievers. *Child and Family Social Work* 7 pp121-130

Martino, W. and Berrill, D. (2003) Boys, Schooling and Masculinities: Interrogating the 'Right' ways to educate boys. *Educational Review* 55 pp 99-117

Maynard, T. (2002) Boys and Literacy: Exploring the issues. London: RoutledgeFalmer

McClelland, N. (1999) *Systems Thinking*. Accessed January, 2006 at: www.literacytrust.org.uk/About/systemic.html

McCrystal, P., Higgins, K. and Percy, A. (2001) Measuring social exclusion: A lifespan approach. *Radical Statistics* 76 Accessed April, 2006 at: http://www.radstats.org.uk/no076/mccrystaletal.htm

McGivney, V. (1999) *Informal Learning in the Community: A Trigger for Change and Development*. Leicester: National Institute for Adult Continuing Education

McLean, N. (2002) Foreword and Introduction to *Digital Divide: A collection of papers from the Toshiba/Becta digital divide seminar*. 19 February, 2002

McNaughton M. J. (1997) Drama and Children's Writing: a study of the influence of drama on the imaginative writing of primary schoolchildren. *Research in Drama Education* 2 (1) pp55-86

Measor, L. and Sikes, P. (1992) Visiting lives: ethics and methodology in life history research, in: Goodson, I. (ed) *Studying Teachers' Lives*. London: Routledge

Miedema, S. and Wardekker, W.L. (1999) Emergent Identity versus Consistent Identity: Possibilities for a postmodern repoliticization of critical pedagogy. In Popkewitz, T.S. and Fendler, L. (eds) *Critical Theories in Education: changing terrains of knowledge and politics*. London: Routledge

Millard, E. (1997) *Differently Literate: Boys, Girls and the Schooling of Literacy*. London: Falmer Press

Moje, E., McIntosh Ciechanowski, K., Kramer, K., Ellis, L., Carrillo, R. and Collazzo, T. (2004) Working towards third space in content area literacy: An examination of everyday funds of knowledge and Discourse. *Reading Research Quarterly* 39 (1) pp 38-70

Moll, L. (2000) Inspired by Vygotsky: Ethnographic experiments in education, in Lee, C. and Smagorinsky, P. (eds) *Vygotskian Perspectives on Literacy Research: Constructing Meaning Through Collaborative Inquiry.* Cambridge, MA: Cambridge University Press

Moll, L., Amanti, C., Neff, D. and Gonzalez, N. (1992) Funds of Knowledge for Teaching: Using a qualitative approach to connect homes and classrooms. *Theory into Practice* 31 pp132-141

Moss, G. (2000) Raising Boys' Attainment in Literacy: some principles for intervention. *Reading* 34 (3) pp101-106

Moss, G. and McDonald, J. (2004) The borrowers: library records as unobtrusive measures of children's reading preferences. *Journal of Research into Reading* 27 (4) pp 401-412

Myhill, D. (2000) Gender and English: Are we wearing the right glasses? *The Secondary English Magazine* 4 (5) pp 25-27

Neelands (1993) *Drama and IT: Discovering the Human Dimension.* London: National Council for Educational Technology

Nesta FutureLab (2005) *The Future of Mobile Technology: Learning 'on the run'?* Vision 1 2005. Accessed February, 2006 at: http://www.digitalstrategy.govt.nz/templates/Page 60.aspx

New London Group (1996) A pedagogy of multiliteracies: Designing social futures. *Harvard Educational Review* 66(1) pp 60-92

Nixon. H. and Comber, B. (1995) Making documentaries and teaching about educational disadvantage: ethical issues and practical dilemmas. *The Australian Educational Researcher* 22(2) pp 63-84

Nixon, H. and Comber, B. (2005) Behind the scenes: making movies in early years class-rooms, in Marsh, J. (ed) P*opular Culture, Media and Digital Literacies in Early Childhood.* London: Routledge/Falmer

Noble, C. and Bradford, W. (2000) *Getting it Right for Boys... and Girls.* London: Routledge

Oakley, K. (2005) *New Zealand Digital Strategy. The Digital Strategy: Creating our Digital Manifesto.* Paper presented at ippr/Yorkshire Forward seminar, Regional Knowledge Economies at the Roud Foundry, Leeds, 26th January 2005

Oakley, K. (2005) *A Sense of Place: The Geography of the Digital Manifesto.* Paper presented at ippr/Yorkshire Forward seminar Regional Knowledge Economies at the Roud Foundry, Leeds, January 2005

Office for Standards in Education (Ofsted) (1996) *The Teaching of Reading in 45 Inner London Primary Schools* (Ref 27/96/D5). London: Her Majesty's Stationery Office

Office for Standards in Education (2003) *Yes He Can: Schools Where Boys Write Well.* London: Her Majesty's Stationery Office

Office for Standards in Education (2004). *Reading for Purpose and Pleasure: An Evaluation of the Teaching of Reading in Primary Schools.* London: Her Majesty's Stationery Office

Office for Standards in Education (2006) *Annual Performance Assessment (APA): Local Authority Children's Services 2005 – Report on Outcomes.* London: Her Majesty's Stationery Office

Official Journal of the European Communities (2001) Council Resolution of 8 October 2001 on e-Inclusion', exploiting the opportunities of the information society for social inclusion

(2001/C 292/02) Accessed January, 2006 at: europa.eu.int/comm/employment_social/knowledge_society/res_eincl_en.pdf

Oliver, M. and Trigwell, K. (2005) Can blended learning be redeemed? *e-learning* 2 (1) pp17-26

Organisation for Economic Co-operation and Development (OECD) (2003) *Reading for Change: Performance and Engagement across Countries: Results from PISA*. Paris: OECD

Paechter, C. F. (2003) Power, bodies and identity: how different forms of physical education construct varying masculinities and femininities in secondary schools. *Sex Education* 3 pp 47-59

Paechter, C. F. (2003) Masculinities and Femininities as Communities of Practice. *Women's Studies International Forum* 26 (1) pp 69-77

Pahl, K. and Rowsell, J. (2005) *Literacy and Education: The New Literacy Studies in the classroom*. London: Paul Chapman

Parker, D. (2002) Show us a Story: An overview of recent research and resource development work at the British Film Institute. *English in Education* 36 (1) pp 38-45

Parsons, S. (2002) *Basic Skills and Crime: Findings from a Study of Adults Born in 1958 and 1970*. London: Basic Skills Agency

Parsons, S. and Bynner, J. (2002) *Basic Skills and Social Exclusion*. London: Basic Skills Agency

Philo, G. and Miller, D. (2000) *Market Killing*. London: Longman

Popkewitz, T. S. and Fendler, L. (eds) *Critical Theories in Education: Changing Terrains of Knowledge and Politics*. London: Routledge

Postman, N. (1994) *The Disappearance of Childhood*. London: Vintage

Powell, R., McIntyre, E. and Rightmyer, E. (2006) Johnny won't read, and Susie won't read either: Reading instruction and student resistance. *Journal of Early Childhood Literacy* 6(1) pp 5-31

Primary National Strategy (PNS)/United Kingdom Literacy Association (UKLA) *Raising Boys' Achievement in Writing*. Reading Primary National Strategy

Prinsloo, M and Stein, P. (2005) 'Down, Up and Round': Setting children up as readers and writers in South African classrooms, in Anderson, J. *et al.* (eds) *Portraits of Literacy across Families, Communities and Schools: Intersections and Tensions*. New Jersey: Lawrence Erlbaum Associates

Quinlivan, K. and Town, S. (1999) Queer as Fuck? Exploring the Potential of Queer Pedagogies in Researching School Experiences of Lesbian and Gay Youth, in Epstein, D. and Sears, J. (eds) *A Dangerous Knowing: Sexuality, Pedagogy and Popular Culture*. London: Cassell

Rappaport, J. (2000) Community narratives: Tales of terror and joy. *American Journal of Community Psychology* 28 (1) pp 1-24

Rees. J. (2001) Making residential care educational care, in British Agencies for Adoption and Fostering (ed) *Nobody Ever Told Us School Mattered: Raising the Educational Attainments of Children in Public Care*. London: British Agencies for Adoption and Fostering

Riesman, C. K. (1993) *Narrative Analysis*. Thousand Oaks, CA: Sage Publications

Rivers, I. (2000) Social exclusion, absenteeism and sexual minority youth. *Support for Learning* 15 (1) pp13-17

Rivers, I. (2001) The Bullying of Sexual Minorities at School: Its nature and long-term correlates. *Educational and Child Psychology* 18 (1) pp33-46

Rockhill, K. (1994) Gender, Language and the Politics of Literacy, in Maybin, J. (ed) *Language and Literacy in Social Practice: A Reader*. Clevedon: Multilingual Matters

Rofes, E. (1995) Making our Schools Safe for Sissies, in Unks, G. (ed) *The Gay Teen: Educational Practice and Theory for Lesbian, Gay and Bisexual Adolescents*. Routledge: New York

Rosenblatt, L. (1976) *Literature as Exploration*. New York: Noble and Noble

Rosenblatt, L. (1978) *The Reader, the Text, the Poem*. Carbondale, Illinois: Illinois University Press

Rowan, L., Knobel, M., Bigum, C., and Lankshear, C., (2002) *Boys, Literacies and Schooling*. Buckingham: Open University Press

Rutherford, J. (1990) A Place Called Home: Identity and the cultural politics of difference, in J. Rutherford (ed.) *Identity, Community, Culture, Difference*. London: Lawrence and Wishart

Saint-Aubin, A. F. (1992) The Mark of Sexual Preference in the Interpretation of Texts: Preface to a homosexual reading. *Journal of Homosexuality* 24 pp 65-88

Schechner, R. (1988) *Performance Theory*. New York: Routledge.

Schultz, K. (2002) Looking Across Space and Time: Reconceptualising literacy learning in and out of school. *Research in the Teaching of English* 36 pp 356-390

Scribner, S. and Coles, M. (1988) Unpacking literacy, in Kingston, E.R., Kroll, B. and Rose, M. (eds) *Perspectives on literacy*. Carbondale, Ill: Southern Illinois University Press

Sharman, F. and Chadwick, B. (1989) *The A – Z Gastronomique: A Traveller's Guide to French Food and Drink*. Bury St Edmunds: Papermac

Sheehy, M. (2005) Can Non-School Literacies be Practiced in School? An Examination of Social Movement Across Contexts from a Time/space Perspective. Unpublished manuscript. Albany: State University of New York Press

Sheehy, M. and Leander, K. (2004) Introduction, in Leander, K. and Sheehy, M. (eds) *Spatialising Literacy Research and Practice*. New York: Peter Lang

Silin, J.G. (2003) Reading, Writing and the Wrath of my Father. *Reading Research Quarterly* 38 (2) pp260-267

Skelton, C. (2001) Male primary teachers and perceptions of masculinity. *Educational Review*, 55, pp195-209

Skinner, D. and Holland D. (1996) Schools and the cultural production of the educated person in a Nepalese Hill community, in Levinson, B., Foley, D. and Holland, D. (eds) *The Cultural Production of the Educated Person: Critical Ethnographies of Schooling and Local Practice*. Albany: State University of New York Press

Smith, S. (2004) The Non-Fiction Reading Habits of Young Successful Boy Readers: Forming connections between masculinity and reading. *Literacy* 38 (1) pp10-16

Social Exclusion Unit (SEU) (2003) *A Better Education for Children in Care: A Social Exclusion Unit Report*. Wetherby, West Yorkshire: Office of the Deputy Prime Minister

Social Exclusion Unit (SEU) (2004) *About Us/Contacts*. Wetherby, West Yorkshire: Office of the Deputy Prime Minister

Social Exclusion Unit (SEU) (2005) *Children in Care Website*. Accessed April, 2006 at: http://www.socialexclusion.gov.uk/page.asp?id=261n

Social Exclusion Unit (SEU) (2005) *Inclusion through Innovation: Tackling Social Exclusion Through New Technologies*. Wetherby, West Yorkshire: Office of the Deputy Prime Minister

Social Services Inspectorate and Ofsted (1995) *The Education of Children who are Looked After by Local Authorities*. London: Her Majesty's Stationery Office

Soja, E.W. (1996) *Thirdspace: Journey to Los Angeles and Other Real-and-Imagined Places.* Malden, MA: Blackwell

Sparkes, J. and Glennister, H. (2002) Preventing Social Exclusion: Education's contribution, in Hills, J., Le Grand, J. and Pichaud, D.(eds) *Understanding Social Exclusion.* Oxford: Oxford University Press

Street, B. (1984) *Literacy in Theory and Practice.* Cambridge: Cambridge University Press

Street, B. (1995) *Social literacies: Critical Approaches to Literacy in Development, Ethnography and Education.* London: Longman

Sumara, D. (1996) *Private Readings in Public: Schooling the Literary Imagination.* New York: Peter Lang

Talburt, S. (2004) Intelligibility and Narrating Queer Youth, in Rasmussen, M. L., Rofes, E. and Talburt Youth , S.(eds) *Sexualities: Pleasure, Subversion, and Insubordination in and Out of Schools.* New York: Palgrave Macmillan

Taylor, D. and Dorsey-Gaines, C. (1988) *Growing Up Literate: Learning from Inner City Families.* Portsmouth, NH: Heinemann

Thomson, P. (2002) *Schooling the Rustbelt Kids: Making the Difference in Changing Times.* Stoke on Trent: Trentham Books

Titus, J. J. (2004) Boy Trouble: Rhetorical framing of boys' underachievement, in *Discourse: Studies in the Cultural Politics of Education* 25 (2) pp 145-169

Trzesniewski, K. H., Moffitt, T.E., Caspi, A., Taylor, A. and Maughan, B. (2006) Revisiting the Association between Reading Achievement and Antisocial Behaviour: New evidence of an environmental explanation from a twin study. *Child Development* 77 (1) p72

Turner, V. W. (1977) *The Ritual Process: Structure and Anti-Structure.* Ithaca: Cornell University Press

Twist, J. (2006) *The year of the digital citizen.* BBC News Online, January 2nd, 2006. Accessed January, 2006 at: http://news.bbc.co.uk/1/hi/technology/4566712.stm.

Tyner, K. (1998) *Literacy in a Digital World: Teaching and Learning in the Age of Information.* New Jersey: Mahwah

United Nations Educational, Scientific and Cultural Organization (UNESCO) (2006) *Global Monitoring Report on Education for All: Literacy for Life.* Paris: Unesco

Vasquez, V. (2004) *Negotiating Critical Literacies with Young Children.* Mahwah: Lawrence Erlbaum Associates

Vershbow, R. (2005) *Transliterature: Can Humanism Transform the Web?* Accessed January, 2006 at: http://www.futureofthebook.org/blog/archives/2005/10/transliterature.html

Vicars, M. (2005) I have a feeling we're not in Kansas anymore: A British gay educator's reconstructed life-history account of school. *Sex Education* 5 (3) pp269-279

Vicars, M. (2006) 'Queer Goings-on': An autoethnographic account of the experiences and a practice of Performing a Queer Pedagogy. *Auto/Biography* 14(1) pp 21-40

Volk, D. (1999) The teaching and the enjoyment and being together...: sibling teaching in the family of a Puerto Rican Kindergartner. *Early Childhood Research Quarterly* 14 pp 5-34

Wagner, B. J. (1994) Drama and Writing, in Purvis, A. (ed) *The Encyclopaedia of English Studies and Language Arts Vol. 1.* New York: National Council of English and Scholastic

Warner, M. (ed) (1993) *Fear of a Queer Planet: Queer Politics and Social Theory.* Minneapolis: University of Minnesota Press

Warrington, M. and Younger, M. with Bearne, E. (2006) *Raising Boys' Achievements in Primary Schools: Towards an Holistic Approach.* Maidenhead: Open University Press

Weaver-Hightower, M.B. (2003a) The 'Boy Turn' in Research on Gender and Education. *Review of Educational Research* 73 (4) pp 471-498

Weaver-Hightower, M.B. (2003b) Crossing the Divide: Bridging the disjunctures between theoretically oriented and practice-oriented literature about masculinity and boys at school. *Gender and Education* 15 (4) pp 407-423

Wells, G. (1987) *The Meaning Makers: Children Learning Language and Using Language to Learn.* Portsmouth, NH: Heinemann

Who Cares? Trust (WCT) (2001) *Right to Read: Promoting the Benefits of Reading to Children and Young People in Public Care: Project Findings and Recommendations for Good Practice.* London: the Who Cares? Trust, the National Literacy Association and the Paul Hamlyn Foundation

Whitelock, D. and Jelfs, A. (2003) Editorial. *Journal of Educational Media,* special issue on Blended Learning, 28 (2-3) pp 99-100

Wilson, A. (2000) There is No Escape from Third Space Theory: Borderline discourse and the 'in between' literacies of prisons, in Barton, D., Hamilton, M. and Ivanic, R. (eds) *Situated Literacies: Reading and Writing in Context.* London: Routledge.

Williams, S. E. (1995) Lapped by girls. *Times Educational Supplement.* 14th July, p5

Williams. R. (1981) *Culture.* Glasgow: Fontana

Wilson, D., Burgess, S. and Briggs, A. (2006) *The Dynamics of School Attainment of England's Ethnic Minorities.* CASE Paper 105. Accessed January, 2006 at: http://sticerd. lse.ac.uk/case/publications/papers.asp

Wilson, S. M., Bell, C., Galosy, J. A. and Shouse, A. W. (2004) 'Them that's got shall get': Understanding teacher recruitment, induction, and retention, in Smylie, M. and Miretsky, D. (eds.) *Teacher Workforce Development. Yearbook of the National Society for the Study of Education* 103(1) pp 145-179

Winterson, J. (1991) *Oranges are Not the Only Fruit.* London: Vantage

Wolcott, H. F. (1994) *Transforming Qualitative Data: Description, Analysis and Interpretation.* London: Sage

Younger, M. and Warrington, M. with Gray, J., Rudduck, J., McLellan, R., Bearne, E., Kershner, R. and Bricheno, P. (2005a) *Raising Boys' Achievement: Research Report No. 636.* London: Department for Education and Skills

Younger, M. and Warrington, M. with McLellan, R. (2005b) *Raising Boys' Achievements in Secondary Schools: Issues, Dilemmas and Opportunities.* Buckingham: Open University Press

Index